HERITAGE AUCTIONS HA.com **BID SHEET**

3500 Maple Avenue | Dallas, Texas 75219-3941
Direct Client Service Line – Toll Free: 866-835-3243 | Fax: 214-409-1425

ALL INFORMATION MUST BE COMPLETED AND FORM SIGNED

CLIENT# (IF KNOWN)   BIDDER#

MW01177882

❏ Mr. ❏ Mrs. ❏ Ms. ❏ Dr. _____
NAME

ADDRESS _____

CITY _____ **STATE** ____ **ZIP CODE** _____ **COUNTRY** _____

EMAIL _____

(COUNTRY CODE) **DAY PHONE** _____ (COUNTRY CODE) **NIGHT PHONE** _____

(COUNTRY CODE) **CELL** _____ (COUNTRY CODE) **FAX** _____

❏ **IF NECESSARY, PLEASE INCREASE MY BIDS BY** ❏1 ❏2 ❏3 **INCREMENT(S)**
Lots will be purchased as much below top bids as possible.

❏ **I WANT TO LIMIT MY BIDDING TO A TOTAL OF $** _____
at the hammer amount for all lots listed on this bid sheet. I am aware that by utilizing the Budget Bidding feature, all bids on this sheet will be affected. If I intend to have regular bidding on other lots I will need to use a separate bid sheet.

Do you want to receive an email, text message, or fax confirming receipt of your bids?
❏ Email   ❏ Cell Phone Text   ❏ Fax

Payment by check may result in your property not being released until purchase funds clear our bank. Checks must be drawn on a U.S. bank. All bids are subject to the applicable Buyer's Premium. See HA.com for details.

I have read and agree to all of the Terms and Conditions of Auction: inclusive of paying interest at the lesser of 1.5% per month (18% per annum) or the maximum contract interest rate under applicable state law from the date of auction.

REFERENCES: New bidders who are unknown to us must furnish satisfactory industry references or a valid credit card in advance of the auction date.

(Signature required) *Please make a copy of this bid sheet for your records.*

❏ I HAVE PREVIOUSLY BOUGHT FROM HERITAGE AUCTIONS

❏ I HAVE A RESALE PERMIT – *please contact 800-872-6467*

Non-Internet bids (including but not limited to, podium, fax, phone and mail bids) may be submitted at any time and are treated similar to floor bids. These types of bids must be on-increment or at a half increment (called a cut bid). Any podium, fax, phone or mail bids that do not conform to a full or half increment will be rounded up or down to the nearest full or half increment and will be considered your high bid.

Current Bid	Bid Increment		
< – $10	$1	$10,000 – $19,999	$1,000
$10 – $29	$2	$20,000 – $29,999	$2,000
$30 – $49	$3	$30,000 – $49,999	$2,500
$50 – $99	$5	$50,000 – $99,999	$5,000
$100 – $199	$10	$100,000 – $199,999	$10,000
$200 – $299	$20	$200,000 – $299,999	$20,000
$300 – $499	$25	$300,000 – $499,999	$25,000
$500 – $999	$50	$500,000 – $999,999	$50,000
$1,000 – $1,999	$100	$1,000,000 – $1,999,999	$100,000
$2,000 – $2,999	$200	$2,000,000 – $2,999,999	$200,000
$3,000 – $4,999	$250	$3,000,000 – $4,999,999	$250,000
$5,000 – $9,999	$500	$5,000,000 – $9,999,999	$500,000
		>$10,000,000	$1,000,000

Bid in whole dollar amounts only.   Please print your bids.

LOT NO.	AMOUNT	LOT NO.	AMOUNT	LOT NO.	AMOUNT

REV. 7-30-13

Last Name: _____

Bid in whole dollar amounts only.   Please print your bids.

LOT NO.	AMOUNT	LOT NO.	AMOUNT	LOT NO.	AMOUNT

Please make a copy of this bid sheet for your records.

Heritage Signature® Auction #7085

The Stan Musial Collection

November 8-9, 2013 | Dallas

Signature® Internet Sessions 1-2
Mail, Fax, Internet & Phone Extended Bidding only*

Session 1 - Sports Cards & Non-Sports Cards
(see separate catalog)
Thursday, November 7 • 10:00 PM CT • Lots 80001-81358

Session 2 - Sports Memorabilia
Friday, November 8 • 10:00 PM CT • Lots 81359 - 82655
(see separate catalog)

The Stan Musial Collection • Lots 81359 - 81568

Sessions 3 Final Session
Mail, Fax, Internet & Extended Bidding only

Session 3 - FINAL SESSION
Saturday, November 9 • 10:00 PM CT • Lots 82656 - 83526
(see separate catalog)

The Stan Musial Collection • Lots 82739 - 82983

LOT SETTLEMENT AND PICK-UP
Weekdays beginning Monday, November 11,
9:00 AM – 5:00 PM CT by appointment only.

This auction is subject to a 19.5% Buyer's Premium.

*Internet & Phone Extended Bidding Session

These sessions presented via catalog and online. Bidding is taken by phone and through our website. There are two phases of bidding during this type of auction:

1) Normal bidding: Bids are taken up until 10 PM CT the night the auction closes.

2) Extended Bidding / 30 Minute Ending: On a lot-by-lot basis, starting at 10:00 PM CT, any person who has bid on the lot previously may continue to bid on that lot until there are no more bids for 30 minutes. For example, if you bid on a lot during Normal Bidding, you could participate during Extended Bidding for that lot, but not on lots you did not bid on previously. If a bid was placed at 10:15, the new end time for that lot would become 10:45. If no other bids were placed before 10:45, the lot would close. If you are the high bidder on a lot, changing your bid will not extend the bidding during the 30 Minute Ending phase (only a bid from another bidder will extend bidding). If you are the only bidder at 10 PM, you will automatically win the lot at 10:30.

Important: After normal bidding ends, you must be signed-on to the Heritage site to see the bidding option on lots where you qualify for extended bidding.

LOT VIEWING
By appointment only. Please contact Mike Provenzale at 214-409-1422 or MProvenzale@HA.com to schedule an appointment.

Heritage Auctions, Dallas • 17th Floor
3500 Maple Avenue • Dallas, TX 75219

Weekdays beginning Monday, October 7 – Friday, November 8
9:00 AM – 5:00 PM CT

View lots & auction results online at HA.com/7085

BIDDING METHODS:

Internet Bidding
Internet absentee bidding ends at 10:00 PM CT the evening before each session. HA.com/7085

Fax Bidding
Fax bids must be received on or before Wednesday, November 6, by 12:00 PM CT. Fax: 214-409-1425

Mail Bidding
Mail bids must be received on or before Wednesday, November 6.

Phone: 214.528.3500 • 800.872.6467
Fax: 214.409.1425
Direct Client Service Line: 866.835.3243
Email: Bid@HA.com

TX Auctioneer licenses: Samuel Foose 11727; Robert Korver 13754; Scott Peterson 13256; Bob Merrill 13408; Mike Sadler 16129; Andrea Voss 16406; Jacob Walker 16413; Stewart Huckaby 16590; Wayne Shoemaker 16600; Chris Dykstra 16601; Teia Baber 16624; Jennifer Marsh 17105; Shawn Schiller 17111; Stephanie O'Barr 17116; Mark Prendergast 17118; Fiona Elias 17126; Brian Nalley 17134; Mike Provenzale 17157.

29997

Steve Ivy
CEO
Co-Chairman of the Board

Jim Halperin
Co-Chairman of the Board

Greg Rohan
President

Paul Minshull
Chief Operating Officer

Todd Imhof
Executive Vice President

Sports Department Specialists

Chris Ivy
Director of Sports Auctions

Derek Grady
Vice President

Rob Rosen
Vice President

Peter Calderon
Consignment Director

Mike Gutierrez
Consignment Director

Mark Jordan
Consignment Director

Tony Giese
Consignment Director

Jonathan Scheier
Consignment Director

Chris Nerat
Consignment Director

Lee Iskowitz
Consignment Director

Calvin Arnold
Consignment Director

3500 Maple Avenue • Dallas, Texas 75219
Phone 214-528-3500 • 800-872-6467
HA.com/Sports

Consignment Directors: Chris Ivy, Derek Grady, Rob Rosen, Peter Calderon, Tony Giese,
Mike Gutierrez, Mark Jordan, Jonathan Scheier, Chris Nerat, Lee Iskowitz, Calvin Arnold

Cataloged by: Jonathan Scheier, Peter Calderon, Chris Nerat, Tony Giese
Derek Grady, Lee Iskowitz

"No man has ever been a perfect ballplayer," Ty Cobb once explained to a Life Magazine journalist. *"Stan Musial, however, is the closest to being perfect in the game today. He plays as hard when his club is away out in front of the game as he does when they're just a run or two behind."* When considering the source of this lofty praise, the sentiment becomes all the more powerful. Both respected and reviled for a fierce competitive drive that made him the most feared hitter of his age, Cobb saw in Musial the only man in the game worthy of carrying his bright-burning torch.

But while Cobb made more enemies than friends over the course of his storied career, Stan Musial enjoys status as one of the most beloved figures in the history of our National Pastime. With both a flair for the dramatic (like his twelfth-inning walk-off homer in the 1955 All-Star Game) and a startling consistency (his 3,630 career hits were divided precisely to 1,815 at home and 1,815 on the road), Stan the Man became arguably the most beloved twentieth century ballplayer who never wore Yankee pinstripes, earning a trio of World Championships and National League MVP Awards in twenty-two seasons of play. For seven full decades, up until the very end of his long life, Stan Musial was the face of the Cardinals franchise. And he'll never be forgotten.

Presented on the pages that follow is a rare opportunity to keep Musial's memory burning brightly in your own trophy room, a vast and varied assortment of personal keepsakes once belonging to the 1969 Hall of Fame inductee and consigned to this auction by the Musial family. The offerings cover the full expanse of The Man's baseball life, from high school to the minor leagues to the Majors and, finally, to Cooperstown immortality and beyond. Each lot will be accompanied by a letter of provenance from the Musial family.

Chris Ivy
Director of Sports Auctions

Letters of Provenance

Lots 81359 - 81538 in Session 2
Lots 82739 - 82983 in Session 3

Each of these lots within this catalog that originate directly from the personal collection of Stan Musial and will be accompanied by a Letter of Provenance from the Musial family as imaged.

Platinum Index

SESSION TWO – THE STAN MUSIAL COLLECTION

Mail, Fax, Internet & Phone Extended Bidding Only Auction #7085
Friday, November 8, 2013 | 10:00 PM CT | Dallas | Lots 81359–81568
Session Two Lots 81569–82655 continue in the Sports Memorabilia Catalog

A 19.5% Buyer's Premium ($14 minimum) Will Be Added To All Lots
To view full descriptions, enlargeable images and bid online, visit HA.com/7085

81359   Stan Musial's Wallet with Contents Including Driver's Licenses, Social Security Cards, More. There are few things more personal than a man's wallet, and Musial's provides no shortage of insight into the great slugger's life. Great value and intrigue in this lot, beginning with the earliest Musial autograph we've encountered, a *"Stanley F. Musial"* model applied to his worn but still solid and complete Social Security card issued to The Man as a sixteen-year old boy. Also here is a 1985 signed Social Security card, autographed the same way. We also have four signed Missouri driver's licenses, expiring in 1988, 1997, 2003 and 2006 respectively. Also a Visa (signed), American Express (unsigned) and Neiman Marcus (signed) credit card. There are nine various health care cards, one with the details of Musial's pacemaker. Also here are two nice cigarette lighters, a couple name badges, a leather box (7x3x2") with Musial's name embossed in gold on lid and a bronze medallion of unknown origin. *Pre-certified by PSA/DNA.*
Starting Bid: $500

81360   1939 Stan Musial Signed High School Yearbook. *Stan the Kid?* It's definitely one of the earliest Musial autographs on the market, applied just to the left of a photo of the high school senior at age eighteen with 8/10 boldness. Listed along with his interest in baseball are basketball and intramural ping pong. His poetic couplet: *"Stan's far more than just an athlete/He's friendly, full of fun, and neat."* We find the slugger on the rise fourth from the left in the top row of the baseball team photo as well, with text below lamenting his loss to the Mountain State League for the start of his professional career. The Donora (PA) High School yearbook is in remarkably fine condition, all but unchanged from its issue during the Baseball Centennial season of 1939. *Pre-certified by PSA/DNA.*
Starting Bid: $500

81361   1941 Babe Ruth Single Signed Baseball Given to Stan Musial as a Minor Leaguer. It was not long before his Major League debut with the St. Louis Cardinals on September 17, 1941 that two greats of the game shared a moment together. One of them ranked among the most famous men in the world. The other was a virtual unknown to the American public, but that was soon to change. Presented is an Official International League (Shaughnessy) baseball signed by Babe Ruth for a twenty-year old outfielder of the Rochester Red Wings, the Double-A farm club of the St. Louis Cardinals with whom Musial would earn his immortality. The sphere exhibits evident game use and a light coating of shellac that has performed its intended duty admirably, preserving the Babe's side panel blue fountain pen ink at an 8/10 level.

This is arguably the most significant Babe Ruth signed baseball to reach the hobby's auction block since a nearly pristine sphere inscribed to Ted Williams commanded a staggering $195,500 in April 2012. *Full LOA from PSA/DNA. Auction LOA from James Spence Authentication.*
Starting Bid: $10,000

81362   1945-46 Stan Musial Game Worn US Navy Baseball Uniform. The young Cardinals superstar bravely enlisted in the defense of his nation on January 23, 1945, and while the turning tide of the Second World War resulted in his assignment to non-combat duties, the horrors of the conflict were never far from Musial's mind. In June of 1945, he was shipped to Hawaii where he would work on a ferry launch unit bringing damaged warships back into the docks of Pearl Harbor, where the Japanese threw down the gauntlet three and a half years earlier to draw the United States into the bloody conflict.

It was in the shadow of the sunken USS Arizona that Musial worked to keep morale high for those sailors and soldiers bound for or returning from the Pacific theater, sporting this road grey flannel uniform that is arguably even more historically significant than the birds and bat models he wore as he charted his path to Cooperstown immortality in the Majors. The design is fittingly sedate for the times, a simple block lettered "Navy" arching across the chest and the unfamiliar number "14" on verso, evidence that Musial got no special treatment, even in the choice of his jersey number. The garment shows strong wear and some scattered staining deriving either from play or storage, but there are no holes, tears or other structural issues. The matching pants are similarly tagged "Wilson [size] 36" at interior waistband and show even stronger evidence of play, with staining from infield clay as well as other effects, and an unrepaired tear in the seat.

In his famous January 1942 "Green Light Letter" to Commissioner Kenesaw Mountain Landis, President Franklin D. Roosevelt made a compelling, and ultimately successful, argument that baseball should continue on in spite of the War, writing in part, *"I honestly feel that it would be best for the country to keep baseball going. There will be fewer people unemployed and everybody will work longer hours and harder than ever before. And that means that they outhg to have a chance for recreation and for taking their minds off their work even more than ever before."* And while the loss to military service of legends like Musial, DiMaggio and Williams certainly altered the level of competition, the dedication of these men to their country strengthened the important belief that all Americans were in this together. Certainly we are unlikely to ever see our modern athletic superstars make a similar sacrifice. And while the jersey could be seen to represent the reason for his absence from the 500 Home Run Club, it is also a tangible tribute, unlike any other, to Musial's famous nickname. *LOA from Heritage Auctions. Letter of provenance from Musial Family.*

Starting Bid: $5,000

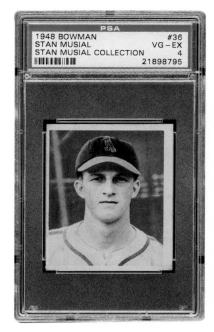

81364 **Stan Musial's Personally Owned 1948 Bowman Rookie #36 Card, PSA VG-EX 4.** It's often been said that one of the greatest rookie thrills is seeing one's face on a trading card for the first time. For the great Stan Musial, it was a thrill that came seven seasons after he first suited up in the uniform of the St. Louis Cardinals, but it's still a rookie card, and still a great thrill. There was only a single example of the important 1948 Bowman #36 card in the vast confines of *The Stan Musial Collection*, and this is it—The Man's one and only personally owned model. It presents even better than its assigned VG-EX rating by PSA, but it's the next line on the service's header that makes this one so special: *"Stan Musial Collection."* The ultimate "population one" card!
Starting Bid: $200

81363 **1945 Stan Musial Worn US Navy Uniform.** Dress blues were owned and worn by the St. Louis Cardinals legend for his term of service to his nation during the Second World War. The heavy navy flannel shirt and matching pants show wear but no damage, presenting perfectly. Musial's signature provides attribution on a tag at rear exterior collar that reads, "Manufactured by Naval Clothing Factory. We find an identical label at interior waistband of the pants, but the handwriting upon it has faded beyond legibility. A fine memento of the patriotism that decimated the talent pool of Major League Baseball but helped to free the world from tyranny during mankind's most important military conflict.
Starting Bid: $2,500

81365 **Circa 1950 St. Louis Cardinals Ballpark Flown Flag Owned by Stan Musial.** One of our favorite lots from The Stan Musial Collection, this massive (42x96") flag is clearly many decades old, and also clearly an official model created for the purpose of display at Sportsman's Park. Our best guess at vintage is circa 1950, and the design of the *"Baldwin Regalia Co., St. Louis, Mo"* label strengthens that theory. The canvas and tackle twill construction has remained solid and complete, and a degree of weathering is only to be expected given its history. As a ballpark-flown relic from the personal collection of the franchise's greatest hero, this is a lot we expect will bring Cardinals collectors out in force.
Starting Bid: $500

81366   Circa 1950 Stan Musial St. Louis Cardinals Traveling Trunk. Perhaps the best of the three Musial trunks in this auction, this one has the legendary slugger's name artfully painted on the side and a St. Louis Cardinals address sticker for Busch Stadium affixed to the top. Wheels on the bottom are fully functional, as are the clasps. Interior has original clothing hangers and drawers. Dimensions are 12x22x36". Manufacturer's emblem from "Priesmeyer Brothers Trunk Co." of St. Louis. Plenty of traveling wear but no damage evident. *Third party shipping required.*
Starting Bid: $250

81367   Circa 1950 Stan Musial St. Louis Cardinals Traveling Trunk. Large steamer trunk almost certainly traveled the National League with the St. Louis Cardinals legend, as this is the type used by the players of his era. Certainly it belonged to him for either professional or personal use, as his name is neatly painted onto its surface. This is a quality trunk with a functioning lock and two keys still present. Interior has multiple wooden drawers on one side, and an open area on the other. Dimensions 21x23x40". *Third party shipping required.*
Starting Bid: $200

81368   Circa 1950 Stan Musial St. Louis Cardinals Traveling Trunk. Baseball's version of Al Capone's vault? Let's hope it's better than that. But one thing's for sure—this ancient shipping trunk painted with Musial's name weighs far, far too much to be empty. The problem? We simply cannot crack it open. We were able to get the lock to pop, but decades of use and storage has provided its own natural locking mechanism—it's absolutely wedged shut. The mind swims with the possibilities, but this is a lot for the gambling soul, as the contents could be anything from jerseys and bats to old newspapers. At the very least, you have a trunk that traveled the National League with one of the greatest hitters of all time. Dimensions 22x25x42". *Third party shipping required.*
Starting Bid: $250

81369   1952 Ty Cobb Handwritten Letter to Stan Musial with Spectacular Content.
Arguably the greatest letter ever written from one ballplayer to another, this lengthy epistle in the Peach's favored green ink provides far too much quote-worthy content to fully supply here, talking batting averages, Williams and DiMaggio, slump busting, and, of course, the evils of the sportswriting profession. But clearly the consistent tone is one of admiration, quite a compliment from a man with a famously rigorous standard for excellence. *"Seriously now, I know well that you averaged in 6 of your last 7 years .355. Does that give you a right to be so darn modest,"* Cobb writes. *"So go out there now and lead the league again and if you don't lead both Major Leagues this year, you should be shot in the behind with mustard seed."*

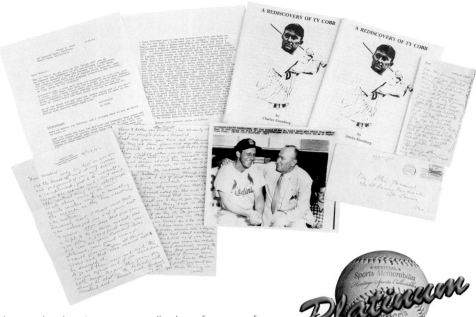

The text covers one side of the first page, both sides of the second, and continues on to a smaller sheet of note paper for one side of a third. The first page is signed *"Ty Cobb,"* with the postscript signed again as *"Ty,"* with the closing suggestion, *"Never change your present style of hitting."* All ink is 9+/10 and pages are in fine condition with original mailing folds. Original mailing envelope is here as well, addressed to *"Mr. Stan Musial, c/o St. Louis Cardinals, St. Louis, Mo."* Full LOA from PSA/DNA.
Starting Bid: $2,500

81370   1950's Stan Musial St. Louis Cardinals Equipment Bag. Heavy canvas bag shows miles upon miles of travel throughout the National League, and one can only imagine the treasure trove of gloves, uniforms and various gear that once resided within. Today the bag is empty of all but the tremendous mystique of its past ownership, a relic that immediately brings The Man to mind with its stenciled number "6" on each end beneath a bold "St. Louis Cardinals." Remarkably, the bag has proved as durable as the man who carried it, with no holes or tears, and a still-functional heavy-duty zipper. Dimensions are approximately 14x12x26".
Starting Bid: $1,000

81371   1950's Stan Musial Game Worn St. Louis Cardinals Pants (2 Pairs). We're quite confident that the fact that these pants were part of Musial's personal collection, and that the are appropriate in size for his build, would indicate that he wore them in competition, but in the interest of full disclosure it must be noted that his name or number does not appear within either pair. It was not uncommon in these days for pants to share owners when one pair was damaged and another had been abandoned as the result of a trade or injury of its original owner. Each is in standard road grey format with "Rawlings" labeling inside the waistband, and size "36" identifiers. Both are likewise tagged to the 1954 season, though it's entirely likely that the use extended beyond that season. One pair has an embroidered attribution to *"G. Staley,"* a pitcher on the 1954 staff. Each pair exhibits solid wear but nothing that could properly characterized as damage. A very rare opportunity to own genuine game worn flannel from the greatest Cardinal of them all. *LOA from Heritage Auctions.*
Starting Bid: $1,000

81372 Early 1960's Stan Musial Game Worn St. Louis Cardinals Cap.
Very heavy wear on this navy blue gamer suggests a complete season of wear at a minimum, though the superstition of the average Big Leaguer certainly opens up the possibility that the dirt and sweat infused into the dark wool is the result of multiple campaigns. We'll also theorize that this is the cap that Stan the Man carried home after clearing out his locker for the last time, and thus the very one that was on his head as he put the last touches on his Hall of Fame resume. The cardboard in the visor is broken in a couple spots but this fact is not apparent except when handled—the aesthetics are not harmed in the slightest. A silver sharpie autograph on the visor exhibits impressive 9/10 boldness. Great wear, great provenance—what more could you want?
Starting Bid: $1,000

81373 Early 1960's Stan Musial Game Worn Spikes. It's been said that the shoes make the man, and surely the same holds true for The Man. These late career spikes carried the Cardinals Hall of Famer for some of his final trips around the bases, quite possibly the very shoes he wore for his final farewells to the game he dominated for over two decades. Each is tagged "Spalding" at interior tongue, where a bold vintage number "6" is applied in black marker. Game worn Musial material is very rare and highly coveted, and the unbeatable provenance that accompanies this offering sets this offering apart from the pack.
Starting Bid: $500

81374 Early 1960's Stan Musial Game Worn Undershirt & Socks. His game worn jerseys cost as much as European sports cars, so this is an attractive alternative for the more budget-conscious collector looking to own a piece of The Man. Best is a heavily worn white undershirt with a vintage "6 Musial" and "6" written on front and back respectively. A pair of white tube athletic socks are unmarked but guaranteed genuine and from Musial's wardrobe.
Starting Bid: $250

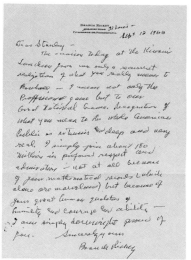

81375 1963 Branch Rickey Handwritten Signed Letter to Stan Musial. A man who knew a thing or two about character, having rescued Major League Baseball from its ugliest fault, pens a letter of admiration to Stan the Man upon his retirement. In part, *"I simply join about 180 million in profound respect and admiration—not at all because of your mathematical records (which alone are marvelous) but because of your great human qualities of humility and courage and ability—I am simply downright proud of you."* On his personal letterhead, he closes, *"Sincerely yours, Branch Rickey."* All ink is 9+/10. Page exhibits original mailing folds but no other faults. Original mailing envelope included. *Pre-certified by PSA/DNA.*
Starting Bid: $500

81376   1960's President Lyndon B. Johnson Signed Photograph to Stan Musial from The Stan Musial Collection. The Commander in Chief and The Man share a private moment in this marvelous black and white image. A bold black ink inscription at the bottom border reads, *"To Stan Musial, my best, Lyndon B. Johnson."* Dimensions 12x15" in original frame. *Pre-certified by PSA/DNA.*
Starting Bid: $250

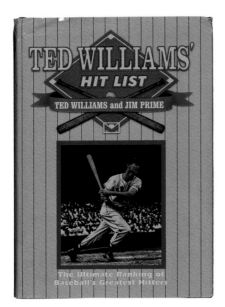

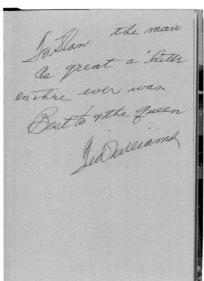

81377   1996 Ted Williams Inscribed & Signed Book to Stan Musial. They racked up 6,284 hits and 996 homers between them, and each ended an All-Star Game with a walk-off blast (in 1941 and 1955 respectively). Though they met only once outside of exhibition contests, in the 1946 World Series, their shared brilliance garnered a mutual respect we find documented in The Splendid Splinter's wonderful inscription: *"To Stan the Man, As great a hitter as there ever was. Best to [you] & the Queen, Ted Williams."* One must assume that the "Queen" was a nickname for Musial's wife Lillian. Dust jacket is a bit rumpled but otherwise book and all writing is NRMT-MT. *Pre-certified by PSA/DNA.*
Starting Bid: $200

81378   2004 Stan Musial Used Shovel & Hard Hat for New Busch Stadium Groundbreaking. Cardinals history meets Cardinals future as the team's greatest living figure participated in the groundbreaking for the team's new ballpark. Presented are the shovel and hard hat used by The Man that day. The former is a charming hybrid of a Louisville Slugger and a polished shovel blade engraved, *"St. Louis Cardinals, Ballpark Groundbreaking, January 2004."* The helmet features logo stickers at front and back.
Starting Bid: $200

81379 2006 Stan Musial Bronze Statue by Sculptor Who Created Busch Stadium Statue. Magnificent study in bronze of the left-handed swing that recorded more hits than all but three men in the history of the Majors is the unmistakable work of Harry Weber, whose life-sized Musial statue holds a place of honor just outside the turnstiles of Busch Stadium. This example might be even more special for being Stan the Man's personal model, and his autograph is carved into the mold that created the casting. Weber's signature and a partially legible edition number is carved into the base. Height is approximately eighteen inches. *Third party shipping required.*
Starting Bid: $1,000

81381 2006 Stan Musial Bronze Statue by Sculptor Who Created Busch Stadium Statue. Magnificent study in bronze of the left-handed swing that recorded more hits than all but three men in the history of the Majors is the unmistakable work of Harry Weber, whose life-sized Musial statue holds a place of honor just outside the turnstiles of Busch Stadium. This example might be even more special for being Stan the Man's personal model, and his autograph is carved into the mold that created the casting. Weber's signature and a partially legible edition number is carved into the base. Height is approximately eighteen inches. *Third party shipping required.*
Starting Bid: $1,000

81380 2006 Stan Musial Bronze Statue by Sculptor Who Created Busch Stadium Statue Plus Smaller Bust. Magnificent study in bronze of the left-handed swing that recorded more hits than all but three men in the history of the Majors is the unmistakable work of Harry Weber, whose life-sized Musial statue holds a place of honor just outside the turnstiles of Busch Stadium. This example might be even more special for being Stan the Man's personal model, and his autograph is carved into the mold that created the casting. Weber's signature and a partially legible edition number is carved into the base. Height is approximately eighteen inches. Also here is a smaller (ten inches tall) bronze bust presented to Musial upon his 1999 recognition as a "Missouri Sports Legend." *Third party shipping required.*
Starting Bid: $1,000

81382 2006 Stan Musial Bronze Statue by Sculptor Who Created Busch Stadium Statue. Only twenty-five examples of this marvelous artwork were cast, and it should come as little surprise that Musial's personal model would be number six from that limited edition. The bronze figural stands twenty-seven inches tall on a 9x14x1.5" slab of marble that adds even more weight to the super-hefty creation. This is a museum-quality creation for sure, with the added appeal of original ownership by The Man himself! Artist is Harry Webber, whose life-sized statue of Musial stands outside Busch Stadium.
Starting Bid: $1,000

81383   **2004 St. Louis Cardinals National League Championship Ring Presented to Stan Musial.** Not even the Curse of the Bambino could save the birds from the Red Sox juggernaut, which first shocked the Yankees by surviving a three-games-to-nothing ALCS deficit before sweeping the World Series to end eighty-six years of misery. Consolation prizes don't get much prettier than this, however, presented to the team's greatest living ambassador for his decades of service to the top dogs of the Senior Circuit. A ruby logo bird is offset by a sea of real diamonds on the face, ringed by the words "*National League Champions Cardinals.*" A bold "*Stan Musial*" appears on left shank above another team logo, while right shank announces "*2004, 16th World Series, 105-57.*" Interior band is stamped "Intergold 14K" and measures to a size ten and a half. Original wood and glass display box is included. NRMT-MT.

Starting Bid: $5,000

81384   **2006 St. Louis Cardinals World Championship Ring Presented to Stan Musial.** Ending the team's longest World Series drought since defeating Babe Ruth's Bronx Bombers in 1926, the red birds earned their tenth World Championship (and their first since 1982) after a dominant five-game performance against the American League pennant-winning Detroit Tigers. Here we find the ultimate symbol of baseball's highest achievement, a stunning and massive Championship ring presented to the greatest living Cardinal of them all, a man who earned three of his own rings as a player.

Identical in style to the one presented to the members of the active roster, this regal creation instantly draws the eye with forty fancy-cut rubies forming the Cardinals logo on a bed of 1.3 carats of genuine diamonds. "*St. Louis Cardinals World Champions*" decorates the perimeter of the face in bold raised lettering. The left shank features a Busch Stadium in miniature and the full name of the ring's iconic presentee. Right shank features the birds and bat team logo, a miniature World Series trophy, and the words "*2006, Tenth World Series Title.*" The interior of the size ten and a half band is stamped "Intergold 14K." Included is its original wood and etched glass hinged display case.

Starting Bid: $10,000

81385 **2011 St. Louis Cardinals World Championship Ring Presented to Stan Musial.** It was perhaps the most dramatic turn-around in the long history of Fall Classic competition, the Cardinals twice battling back from their final strike to even the Series at three games apiece, then winning Game Seven to earn rings such as the one offered here. The ultimate symbol of Yogi Berra's famous quotation, *"It ain't over 'til it's over,"* this glimmering keepsake once belonged to the greatest Cardinal of them all.

A red ruby cardinal perches on a golden bat on a field of diamonds adorning the face of the ring, sandwiched between bold text announcing *"World"* and *"Champions."* Left shank provides a three-dimensional *"Stan Musial"* above a ruby filled *"St.L"* logo and the Hall of Famer's retired number *"6."* The first five of eleven World Championship seasons are listed below, completed on the right shank beneath text announcing *"2011 St. Louis Cardinals"* and a ruby-filled number *"11,"* the tally of World Championships for the franchise. Interior band of the white gold beauty is stamped *"Jostens 14K,"* and engraved with the results of the various playoff series, along with the phrase *"Happy Flight,"* a reference to a team policy of winning on the road. Ring is displayed in its original cherry wood and etched glass hinged display case.

Starting Bid: $10,000

81386   2010 President Barack Obama Signed Photograph to Stan Musial. Image was snapped just moments after President Obama placed the Medal of Freedom around Musial's neck, America's highest civilian honor meant to recognize "an especially meritorious contribution to the security or national interests of the United States, or to world peace or to cultural or other significant public or private endeavors." A bold black felt tip inscription in the wide white lower border reads, *"To Stan 'The Man' Musial—Thanks for playing the game the way it's supposed to be played! Barack Obama."* Photo measures 8x10". *Pre-certified by PSA/DNA. Auction LOA from James Spence Authentication.*

Starting Bid: $250

81387   Baseball Hall of Fame Construction Brick Display Presented to Stan Musial. Extravagantly displayed keepsake is best described by the engraved plaque affixed within the glass and cherry wood hinged case: *"The National Baseball Hall of Fame and Museum, Dedicated June 12, 1939, Cooperstown, New York, Presented to Stan Musial whose Hall of Fame plaque symbolizing his greatness as a player was dedicated in 1969. This brick is from the original building and was preserved during the Hall of Fame's 2002-2005 renovation."* Display case is in the shape of a home plate, and measures 15x16x4" at its largest dimensions. Fine condition.

Starting Bid: $500

81388   Stan Musial Signed Checks Lot of 2,339. An enormous volume of high-grade autograph exemplars, and an intriguing research project that provides a never-before-available view into the legendary slugger's personal finances. With very few exceptions the checks appear in fine condition with 9+/10 ink and signed at the close with the rare and desirable *"Stanley Musial"* signature format. Also here, and not included in the official count, are 194 signed by Musial's wife Lillian. A recent sale on eBay for a single Stan Musial check topped $85, so you can see the great investment potential here. *Full LOA from PSA/DNA.*

Starting Bid: $2,500

STAN MUSIAL BATTING TITLE TROPHY BATS

The following three lots rank among the most important relics of *The Stan Musial Collection*, the Cardinals legend's personal trophies for posting the highest batting average in the National League. The tradition of awarding a Silver Bat for the accomplishment would make its debut with Jackie Robinson in 1949, just a year after Musial claimed his third and final batting title. Until that time there had been no official prize for the elite achievement, and so these personal model bats were fashioned into trophies in order to address that deficiency. Each features the same 1948-49 labeling style, suggesting that all three were awarded at one time, either by the St. Louis Cardinals or by the Hillerich & Bradsby bat company. Musial's remarkable stat line, with red stars marking each League-leading figure, is neatly inked on the barrel.

81389   1943 Stan Musial National League Batting Title Presentational Bat. In just his second full season, the twenty-two year old from Donora, Pennsylvania put the baseball world on notice that something truly remarkable was happening in St. Louis. The evidence of Musial's offensive dominance appears on the back of the barrel of the presented bat, with red stars underscoring the National League-leading marks of 220 hits, forty-eight doubles and twenty triples to accompany his .357 average. *Pre-certified by PSA/DNA.*
Starting Bid: $1,000

81390   1946 Stan Musial National League Batting Title Presentational Bat. It's a Cardinals season best remembered for Enos Slaughter's Game Seven "Mad Dash," but without the eye-popping tallies recounted on this trophy bat, the Brooklyn Dodgers surely would have overcome the two-game deficit in the chase for the National League flag. The Man notched a .365 average to lead the Senior Circuit, and red stars appear under his totals for at-bats (624), runs scored (124), hits (228), doubles (50) and triples (20) to denote leading numbers for these as well. Minimal wear to the lettering is apparent, as is some residue on the front barrel, but these are minor distractions. *Pre-certified by PSA/DNA.*
Starting Bid: $1,000

81391   1948 Stan Musial National League Batting Title Presentational Bat. It's considered the greatest season in Stan Musial's career, and the opinion is nearly impossible to dispute, with National League and career-best numbers for average (.376), hits (230), runs scored (135), runs batted in (131), slugging (.702) and total bases (429). Red stars underscore the various staggering tallies on the back barrel. A couple drips of white paint appear on the front barrel, which may be removable but cause little distraction. *Pre-certified by PSA/DNA.*
Starting Bid: $1,000

81392   1943 Stan Musial 200th Hit Baseball. The earliest milestone ball in *The Stan Musial Collection*, dating to his first of three National League MVP and seven batting title seasons. The Man would record an eye-popping 220 hits in 1943, but this was his thirty-third, bringing his career tally to an even 200. The ONL (Frick) ball exhibits solid use from that historic contest at Sportsman's Park, where the Cards were blanked six to nothing by the visiting Chicago Cubs. Who could have imagined that 3,430 hits were still to come?
Starting Bid: $1,000

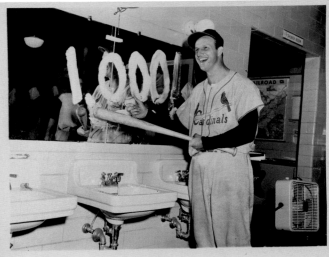

81394   1952 Stan Musial 1,000th Run Batted In Baseball with Photograph. An eighth inning long ball at Ebbets Field off Dodgers ace Joe Black on September 12, 1952 enhanced The Man's four-for-five evening and flipped the fourth digit on his RBI odometer in the eight to five loss to the eventual National League Champs. Presented is the very ONL (Giles) ball that Musial was somehow able to retrieve from beyond the outfield wall, and a vintage 12x14" photo in the visitor's dressing room finds Musial posing with the bat and ball in front of the number *"1,000!"* written in shaving cream on the bathroom mirror. The ball shows strong use from the historic moment, with a vintage *"1000"* penned on the ball's stamping. No other writing. A major milestone en route to baseball immortality.
Starting Bid: $1,000

81393   1949 Stan Musial 24th Home Run of the Season Baseball.
Long a favorite of the left-handed slugger, the short right field porch of the New York Giants' home ballpark paid dividends for the Cardinals legend this day, as he launched his twenty-fourth homer of the 1949 season, and the 134 of his Hall of Fame career. Here's the ONL (Frick) ball that cleared the wall, showing solid use and bearing a vintage side panel notation: *"Stan Musial, 24th Home Run, 27 Aug 1949, Polo Grounds."* This was the first of two long balls delivered to Musial's bat by Giants southpaw Dave Koslo in this first game of a Manhattan doubleheader.
Starting Bid: $1,000

81395   1952 Stan Musial 2,000th Hit Baseball. A fourth-inning single against Philadelphia Phillies southpaw Curt Simmons at Shibe Park established The Man as the first of three left-handed batters in Cardinals history to reach this vaunted milestone. It would prove to be Musial's sole hit in five at-bats that Tuesday night, but it extended his hitting streak to fourteen games, a fact that is noted on the side panel of the historic ONL (Giles) sphere. All of the details of the achievement are neatly penned on various panels of the ball, with a green ink *"Stan 2000th"* over the presidential stamping likely applied in the dugout immediately after the hit in order to provide quick identification. The thirty-one year old slugger would conclude the season with his sixth National League batting title with a splendid .336 final average.

Starting Bid: $2,500

81396   1954 Stan Musial Twentieth Home Run in Fifty Games Baseball. He'd terrified opposing managers for well over a decade when this remarkable power surge battered National League pitching, but never before had there been a better case for the intentional walk when the provided ONL (Giles) ball was served up by Brooklyn Dodgers ace Carl Erskine to Musial's thunderous Louisville Slugger. The neatly notated side panel tells the story: *"Stan Musial's souvenir ball, his 20th H.R. ball in 50 games in 1954 off: Erskine, Tues: June 8th, '54."* Further writing adorns two other panels with details of the ten to three victory at Busch Stadium. An exciting relic from a span that equaled Babe Ruth's torrid 1927 pace.

Starting Bid: $1,000

81397   1957 Stan Musial National League Consecutive Games Record Game Used Baseball. Like the Iron Horse before him, Musial lived up to his own famous nickname with remarkable durability and force of will, topping 1930's Pittsburgh Pirates first baseman Gus Suhr's record with his 823rd consecutive appearance in a National League contest. The presented ONL (Giles) sphere was in operation for that meeting of the Cardinals and the Philadelphia Phillies at Connie Mack Stadium on June 12, 1957. Musial graciously gives a nod in his lengthy notations to his seventeen-year old teammate Von McDaniel, who *"pitched dazzling ball for 4 innings"* in his Major League debut. Musial would ultimately extend the streak to 895 games in August of that year, a mark that still stands as number eight in Major League history. *Auction LOA from James Spence Authentication.*

Starting Bid: $1,000

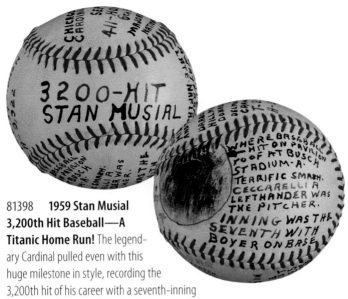

81398   1959 Stan Musial 3,200th Hit Baseball—A Titanic Home Run! The legendary Cardinal pulled even with this huge milestone in style, recording the 3,200th hit of his career with a seventh-inning home run blast off Chicago Cubs southpaw Art Ceccarelli on September 20, 1959 that rattled the pavilion roof of Busch Stadium before settling back into the outfield grass. A red circle is drawn around the dark scuff the ONL (Giles) ball suffered in the collision beside a notation identifying the cause of the bruise. The other panels feature further neatly penned lettering that note the details of the game and the significance of the achievement, stating that this 411th career home run was sixth best in Major League history, and second in the National League.
Starting Bid: $1,000

81400   1962 Stan Musial 1,860th RBI Baseball, Ties Mel Ott. He was recently knocked from the top five on the all-time Major League leaderboard for runs batted in by fellows named Barry Bonds and Alex Rodriguez, so many among us will still count Stan the Man on the single hand of baseball's most prolific run producers. Here we find the ball that drew him even with a slugging legend, as the extensive notations on the provided ONL (Giles) sphere indicates. *"Tied record of Mel Ott with a two base hit scoring Javier in the fifth inning. Pitcher Stan Williams was the victim. Musial's 2 for 3 gave him the League batting lead with a .351 average."* The ball exhibits solid use from the July 24, 1962 meeting with the Los Angeles Dodgers at Busch Stadium. Included is a vintage photo of Musial recording the hit, 10x12".
Starting Bid: $1,000

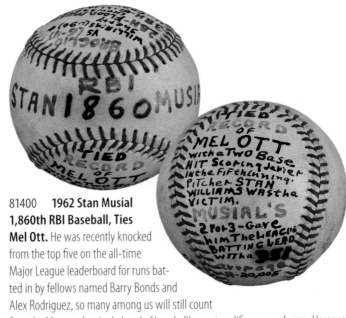

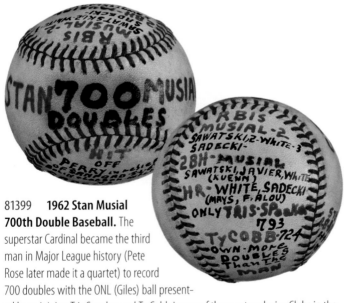

81399   1962 Stan Musial 700th Double Baseball. The superstar Cardinal became the third man in Major League history (Pete Rose later made it a quartet) to record 700 doubles with the ONL (Giles) ball presented here, joining Tris Speaker and Ty Cobb in one of the most exclusive Clubs in the sport. His victim was none other than fellow future Hall of Famer Gaylord Perry, who had come in as relief for San Francisco Giants right-hander Jack Sanford, who would take the loss in this June 9, 1962 contest. Musial would improve his batting average to a lofty .340 in his two-hit performance this day, remaining firmly in the race for the National League batting title at age forty-one (though he'd ultimately finish third). Like the other game used baseballs in The Stan Musial Collection, neat period handwriting details all pertinent information about the achievement, and the ball exhibits expected wear from its date with baseball history.
Starting Bid: $1,000

81401   Stan Musial Signed Dollar Bills Lot of 100 & Unsigned $2 Bills Uncut Sheet. You're already at $132 in value before Musial enters into the equation! Best is a bag of one hundred dollar bills folded into origami rings and autographed by Musial in bold sharpie. He used to give these away to fans. Also here is a sheet of sixteen uncut two dollar bills, still in its Department of the Treasury folder, unsigned. *Pre-certified by PSA/DNA. Auction LOA from James Spence Authentication.*
Starting Bid: $100

81402   Stan Musial Signed Dollar Bills Folded into Rings Lot of 210. The reality is as un-usual as the title, but it serves as living proof of Musial's generosity and fun-loving nature. A marriage of autographed memorabilia and legal tender origami, these rings number 210 in quantity. All autographs are rendered in 9/10 and better blue and black sharpie. Big breakdown value here. *Pre-certified by PSA/DNA. Auction LOA from James Spence Authentication.*
Starting Bid: $500

81403   Stan Musial Signed Dollar Bills Folded into Rings Lot of 200. The reality is as un-usual as the title, but it serves as living proof of Musial's generosity and fun-loving nature. A marriage of autographed memorabilia and legal tender origami, these rings number 200 in quantity. All autographs are rendered in 9/10 and better blue and black sharpie. Big breakdown value here. *Pre-certified by PSA/DNA. Auction LOA from James Spence Authentication.*
Starting Bid: $500

81404   Stan Musial Signed Dollar Bills Folded into Rings Lot of 200. The reality is as un-usual as the title, but it serves as living proof of Musial's generosity and fun-loving nature. A mar-riage of autographed memorabilia and legal tender origami, these rings number 200 in quantity. All autographs   are rendered in 9/10 and better blue and black sharpie. Big breakdown value here. *Pre-certified by PSA/DNA. Auction LOA from James Spence Authentication.*
Starting Bid: $500

81405   1970's Stan Musial Match Used Golf Bag with Six Clubs. Heavy use on this red leather golf bag personalized to the Cardinals great with *"Stan Musial, 'Stan the Man' Inc."* text on the front. A couple personalized tags still affixed to the bag are present, one relating to a 1974 tournament in Florida. The bag contains six period clubs (of which four, oddly, are putters), all correct for Musial's left-handed stance. Manufacturer's emblem is by "Burke-Worthington."
Starting Bid: $200

81406   1970's Stan Musial Match Used Golf Bag & Driver. Heavy use on this Wilson bag with an awesome customization reading *"Stan Musial, St. Louis, Mo., Stan the Man."* The lettering has begun to come loose from years of wear. There's still a driver in the bag, correct for Musial's left-handed style. Various tags from country clubs and airline travel remain affixed.
Starting Bid: $150

81407 1980's Stan Musial Game Used Golf Bag with Two Clubs. Custom "Wilson" bag features bold "Stan Musial, St. Louis, Mo." on the side and bag tags from his local "Sunset Country Club" and his 1987 charity golf tournament with a great caricature of Musial in the design. Bag shows considerable wear from use and travel, and still contains a putter and driver in Musial's left-handed style.
Starting Bid: $200

81409 1990's Stan Musial Game Used Golf Bag & Clubs. High-quality leather bag with "Michelob" beer design features is one of The Man's later models, bearing a St. Louis Cardinals sticker with his name written in marker for identification, and a player badge with his engraved name for a benefit tournament in 1992. Nine clubs remain in the bag, but we must note that three are right-handed drivers, thus clearly not used by Musial. The others are correct for his left-handed stance. All clubs show strong use, with wear on the bag lighter but still clearly evident.
Starting Bid: $250

81408 1980's Stan Musial Game Used Golf Bag & Clubs. High-quality leather bag with "Stan Musial" design on front in white lettering is one of The Man's later models, bearing "Bay Hill Club" guest tag with his name written in marker for identification, "Nemacolin Club" tag with his name printed and a "Major League Baseball Players Alumni" tag with his name written. Four woods are included and each are correct for his left-handed stance. All clubs show strong use, with wear on the bag lighter but still clearly evident.
Starting Bid: $250

81410 1990's Stan Musial Match Used Golf Bag & Clubs. High-quality black leather golf bag bears Michelob beer advertising graphics and plenty of evident wear from the links with a guy who still knew how to hit a ball, even in his golden years. "Stan Musial" is painted on the front of the bag and several badges and tags personalized to the Cardinals slugger are still affixed. Six used clubs remain inside the bag, but we report one is a right-handed model and thus not Stan's personal driver.
Starting Bid: $200

81411   2000's Stan Musial Game Used Golf Bag & Clubs. High-quality cloth bag is one of The Man's later models, bearing an "Old Warson Country Club" name tag tag for identification, and a player badge with his engraved name for a benefit tournament in 2005. Eleven clubs (nine "Callaway Big Bertha") remain in the bag, each consisting of Musial's proper left-handed stance. All clubs show solid use, with wear on the bag also clearly evident.
Starting Bid: $250

81413   Stan Musial Harmonica & Harmonica Club Vest. Musial scholars are well aware that the Cardinals legend played a mean harmonica, and we have one of his personalized models (facsimile signature on a Hohner brand). Also here is a vest he wore as the most famous member of the "Gateway Harmonica Club." Both pieces are in fine condition.
No Minimum Bid

81414   Circa 1960 Stan Musial Signed Magazine Lot of 20. Never one to turn away an autograph request, Stan Musial carefully signed each of these twenty magazines in felt tip ink. Most of the publications are EX to EX/MT with a few lesser. Two covers are detached. *Pre-certified by PSA/DNA. Auction LOA from James Spence Authentication.*
No Minimum Bid

81412   Stan Musial Bowling Ball Bag. Custom hand-crafted leather bag features a St. Louis Cardinal logo bird mowing down the pins beneath a tooled "Stan." The zipper needs to be resewn to the opening of the bag, but otherwise there are no flaws worthy of note beyond a few light spots from handling.
Starting Bid: $100

81415   Famous Athletes & Authors Signed Books to Stan Musial Lot of 6 & More. A thrilling assembly of volumes from Musial's personal library. 1) James Michener signed (not personalized) "Sports in America." 2) Bob Feller personalized "The Baseball Player." 3) James Michener personalized "Mexico." 4) Arnold Palmer personalized "Complete Book of Putting." 5) Tom Wheatley personalized "Mark McGwire 70." 6) Arnold Palmer & Stan Musial signed page in the book "The King and I," essentially a dual-signed photo. 7-9) Three Stan Musial signed copies of "The Man Stan Musial, Then and Now." 10) Kenesaw Landis secretarially signed "1943 Baseball." Signatures average 9/10. *Pre-certified by PSA/DNA.*
Starting Bid: $250

81416   1939 Stan Musial High School Varsity Baseball & Basketball Letter Certificate. One of the earliest pieces of Musial sports memorabilia in existence is presented here, the very certificate that bestowed the Donora (PA) High School varsity letter upon the burgeoning legend. Certificate is signed by his coach and various administrators (not by Musial himself). Vertical center storage fold and wear at edges, but otherwise strong. Dimensions 8.5x11".
Starting Bid: $100

81417   1948-62 Stan Musial Personal Awards and Proclamations Lot of 7. Stan Musial was a pretty busy man during his life. Of course he was hounded at every turn during his career, but even afterwards Musial was a popular subject. Given his cheery disposition, Musial found countless awards and honors coming his way. Each of these proclamations and honors were given to Stan the Man during his playing career. Featured are: 1949 Pennsylvania Ambassador MVP, 1956 Junior Chamber of Commerce, 1958 American Airlines Inc. Admiral of the Flagship Fleet, 1961 Man of The Month Award from Advertising Club of St. Louis, The Missouri Society of New York Mule Award (chipping on matte), 1958 Americanism Award from the American Legion of Milwaukee and 2003 Stan Musial Day in St. Louis.
Starting Bid: $100

81418   1950's-2010's Stan Musial Awards Lot. Best here is the Cardinals line-up card from Musial's final game on September 29, 1963, framed with a Perez-Steele postcard. Also here is an assembly of items commemorating the naming of The Stan Musial Bridge in 2012, namely a certificate from Congressman Mark S. Critz, a signed certificate of recognition from the Baseball Hall of Fame regarding the event, a copy of the bill naming the bridge, with the pen that signed the bill. Next, a letter from the Illinois Secretary of State to Musial regarding his induction to the Polish National Alliance, five certificates of recognition from various sources. Also a Wilson sporting goods sign noting his 1951 All-Star team appearance, two 1987 Old Timers Game presentational plates, and a silver-toned box empty *"Presented to Stan Musial In Honor of the Many Unforgettable Memories Bestowed Upon the City of St. Louis."*
Starting Bid: $250

81419   1950's-90's Stan Musial Awards Lot of 12. An intriguing supply of presentational trophies and awards from Musial's mantel.

1) 1971 Musial & Biggies [Restaurant] plaque in thanks for scoreboard donation to Christian Brothers College. 2-3) Brian P. & Bob Burns Nostalgia Award (two different). 4-6) St. Louis University "The Associates of the President" medallions (two different, each engraved with name on verso). 7) 1980 Nebraska Baseball Digest Man of the Year. 8)1985 St. Louis Association for Retarded Citizens award box. 9) 1950 St. Louis Zone Big Leaguers Campaign by Chevrolet trophy desk clock. 10) 1990 Gateway Harmonica Club trophy. 11) 1999 Stan Musial Omaha Classic award. 12) Stan Musial signed mounted gold Hall of Fame plaque postcard. Average EX condition.
Starting Bid: $250

81420   1959-82 Stan Musial Personal Awards Lot of Five. Given his larger than life status, Stan the Man was bestowed with countless awards and gifts from fans and well-wishers. Acquired directly from the Stan Musial Collection are these five artifacts. Included are: 1.) 2000 Stan Musial Stadium Dedication European Leadership Training Center Kutno, Poland. A detached oversized Little League Baseball ring comfortably sets onto a wood base. 2.) To Stan Musial My Personal Gratitude 11-11-72 drinking mug. 3.) 1959 KXOK Mrs. Missouri Judge plate (some pitting). 4.) 1994 Stan Musial Walk of Fame Tampa Bay award. 5.) 1982 Cardinals Affiliate wood card case with the original pencil.
Starting Bid: $100

81421   1963 Stan Musial Awards & Proclamations Given During His Final Major League Season Lot of 7. It is common practice for sports fans to pay tribute to a select few athletes when they know it will be the last time the player will be performing in front of them. While most legends play until their jersey is virtually ripped from their being, some players know when it is time to call it a career. In July of 1963, Musial let the higher ups know of his decision to retire. Each of these proclamations was issued in 1963, Musial's final big league year. Most measure in the 16x20" range and are framed. Included are: Saint Louis University Stan Musial Field, Musial being commissioned as a Flying Colonel by Delta Airlines, Chamber of Commerce of Greater Pittsburgh Certificate of Recognition, Musial honored in The Old Grand-Dad Club (he became a grandpa in '63), St. Louis City Council gratitude resolution, State of Arkansas Traveler and resolution from the Fourth Annual Baseball Gang Dinner of the San Francisco Press and Union League Club.
Starting Bid: $100

81422   1963-84 Stan Musial Presentational Trophies Lot of 6. Post-career selections from Musial's bulging trophy case. 1) "To My Idol, Stan Musial, 1941-1963." 2&3) "Drive Against Cancer 1972." 4) "Stan Musial & Biggies 'Century Scouter,' St. Louis Area Council, 1975." 5) "The Musial 1983 Winner." 6) "The Musial 1984 Winner." Trophies range from seven to twelve inches in height. A couple are missing the bat or golf club, but otherwise all in fine, displayable condition.
Starting Bid: $100

81423   1960's-90's Stan Musial Non-Baseball Awards Lot of 6. The Hall of Fame slugger is recognized for all manner of achievement, from Christmas season home lighting (1963) to supporting the Jerry Lewis Telethon (1982) to twenty years of service as Director of the Brentwood Bank (1977). Each piece presents in fine condition. Four of the six awards bear Musial's name, but all were presented to him.
Starting Bid: $200

81424   1966-2006 Stan Musial Silver Presentational Plates Lot of 3. Trio of silver plates, as follows. 1) 1966 All-Star Baseball Game presented by Chrysler Corporation. 2) 1968 World Series presented by Chrysler Corporation. Pewter construction. 3) 2006 St. Louis Cardinals World Champions presented by team. Musial's name is not present on any, but these are his personal keepsakes. Average twelve inches in diameter. Minor handling/storage wear, but all present very well.
Starting Bid: $100

81425   1968-81 Stan Musial Presentational Silver Bowls Lot of 2. A pair of silver bowls commemorates special events. Engraved as follows. 1) *"Stan 'The Man' Musial, In Appreciation for Your Visit Honoring Our State Championship Baseball Team, Cumberland, Rhode Island, July 30, 1968."* Height five inches, diameter ten inches. 2) "Presented to Stan Musial in Honor of the 1981 Stan Musial Amateur World Series." Height two and a half inches, diameter five inches. Both are in fine, undamaged condition with minimal tarnishing.
Starting Bid: $75

81426   1968 St. Louis Cardinals National League Championship Black Bat. Stan the Man's personal example of this highly collectible lumber issued to players and VIP's for each World Series squad. Minimal handling wear here—this is one of the nicer examples you'll find, with the added appeal of its former ownership. Thirty-five inches.
Starting Bid: $100

81427   1971 Stan Musial Presentational "East-West All-Stars" Carafe & Glass. Glass and silverplate vessel commemorating the East West All-Stars at Riverfront Stadium. There is some tarnish and minor finish loss to the piece, but otherwise it is in good condition. Engraved, *"East-West All-Stars, Riverfront Stadium—Cincinnati, Stan Musial, June 19, 1971."* Height twelve inches. Also here is a glass and silver vessel, possibly related, unengraved. Height seven inches.
Starting Bid: $100

81428   1972 Stan Musial Presentational Silver Tray from Cardinals/Yankees Reunion. Elegantly crafted silver tray with reticulated edge decor was presented to Musial for a reunion game played on July 9, 1972 between the Cardinals and Yankees at Busch Stadium in St. Louis. Tray measures 22x16" and is engraved to Musial at the center panel. *"Wm. Rogers & Son"* maker's mark on verso. Fine condition.
Starting Bid: $200

81429   1970's-90's Stan Musial Presentational Wristwatches Lot of 4. A quartet of timepieces presented to Musial for various baseball events. 1) Lucien Piccard gold-plated wristwatch engraved *"Old Timers Day, Dodgers 1972"* on verso. 2) Seiko digital wristwatch engraved *"Adios 1981"* on front. 3) Baume & Mercier wristwatch engraved *"50th All Star Game, Chicago White Sox, Baume & Mercier, Henry Kay Jewelers"* on verso. 4) Bulova wristwatch with Baseball Hall of Fame logo on face, engraved *"A Tribute: May 12-13, 1993"* on verso. All are in fine condition, in original packaging.
Starting Bid: $200

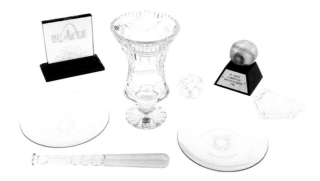

81430   1980's-90's Stan Musial Crystal Presentational Awards & Gifts.
Gorgeous selection of valuable crystal artifacts given to the Cardinals great. 1)
1992 Hall of Fame induction plate. 2) 1993 Hall of Fame induction plate. 3) 1994
Hall of Fame induction vase. 4) Circa 1990 presentational crystal "plaque" from
Boatmen's Bank. 5) Crystal mini-bat from Del Peres Hospital. 6) Waterford crystal
baseball, no engraving. 7) Waterford crystal St. Louis Cardinals logo, no engraving.
8) St. Louis Cardinals 1986 Old Timer's Presentational pewter baseball. All in fine,
undamaged condition.
Starting Bid: $200

**81432   Presentational Awards & Medals from The Stan Musial
Collection.** Another sampling of presentational pieces from the jam-packed
trophy case of Musial's home. 1) Key to the City of Las Vegas, no Musial engraving.
2) Senator John Heinz History Center Medal of Innovation, engraved to Musial. 3)
1968 Brotherhood/Sisterhood Award medal, engraved to Musial. 4) Key to the
City of Kosciusko, Mississippi, no Musial engraving. 5-11) Seven medals, none
engraved, presented to Musial by organizations ranging from the Special Olympics
to the Missouri Athletic Club Hall of Fame. 12) Key to the City of Niigata, Japan,
no Musial engraving. 13) Polish presentational medal of unknown relevance (due
to language). 14-16) Three small presentational pins, none engraved. 17) 1988
Funeral booklet. Fine condition throughout.
Starting Bid: $200

**81431   Stan Musial Golden Anniversary Presentational Wristwatch
& Hall of Fame Pins from The Stan Musial Collection.** Best here is a gold-
colored Seiko quartz wristwatch engraved on verso, "50 Years, Stan Musial World
Series in Battle Creek, MI 1991." The balance of the offering is comprised of Hall of
Fame pins created to commemorate past induction ceremonies. Years represented:
1948, 1954 (2), 1961 (2), 1971 (2), 1979. All contents of lot are in NRMT condition.
Starting Bid: $200

**81433   1996 Little League Baseball's Tribute to Stan Musial Crystal
Trophy.** Weighty and artfully crafted crystal award finds the legendary slugger
standing beside a youngster in fond emulation of his hero. Text on base reports,
*"Little League Baseball's Tribute to Stan Musial, Wednesday, April 10, 1996, St. Louis.,
Missouri."* Height is eleven inches, weight over twenty-one pounds. Fine condition.
Starting Bid: $150

81434   1996 Hall of Fame Induction Presentational Bat. Reserved only for Hall of Famers and VIP's, these bats are created by Louisville Slugger to commemorate the big day at Cooperstown. Green engraved signatures are the new inductees, and the gold are for the past inductees in attendance. Similar in design to the popular "black bats" created for Championship teams. Length thirty-four inches. Mint condition.
Starting Bid: $250

81435   2002 Hall of Fame Induction Presentational Bat. Reserved only for Hall of Famers and VIP's, these bats are created by Louisville Slugger to commemorate the big day at Cooperstown. Similar in design to the popular "black bats" created for Championship teams. This one was surely particularly special to Musial, as the inductee was fellow Cardinals legend Ozzie Smith. Length thirty-four inches. Mint condition.
Starting Bid: $250

81436   1945 Stan Musial United States Navy Worn Uniform Shirt. The Cardinals great enlisted in the military on January 23, 1945 and was soon assigned to special services in Hawaii, where he worked a ferry launch unit to bring back damaged ship crews entering Pearl Harbor, with time to play in the eight-team Navy baseball league in the afternoons. This lightweight canvas shirt was part of Musial's wardrobe during his World War II service, and we find his handwritten name in marker at interior hem. Fine condition with evident wear.
Starting Bid: $500

81437   World War II & Vietnam Militaria from The Stan Musial Collection. The Hall of Fame slugger's noble service to our nation is documented in this expansive lot. Among the highlights: 1) Two Musial signed caps from a pair of USS warships. 2) A photograph album containing images of the attack on Pearl Harbor as well as hunting photos from a Musial excursion and professional photos of his Cardinals teammates. 3) A leather bag and five military pins from Musial's USO mission to Vietnam. 4) Musial notice of classification letters, registration certificate, order to report letter from Selective Services and various patches and medals from his WWII service. 5) A couple dozen photos of Musial and his environment on duty at Pearl Harbor. 6) A personalized to Musial book from US Naval Training Center in 1968. 7) Musial's 1944 "The Bluejackets Manual" issued to him upon enlistment. 8) A couple dozen snapshot photos of the Navy baseball team with several Musial shots. 9) A Navy training film reel. 10) A presentational Navy pen. *Pre-certified by PSA/DNA.*
Starting Bid: $200

81438   1945-46 Stan Musial US Navy Foot Locker. During The Man's noble service to our nation during the Second World War, this rather rustic wooden box was his daily companion, containing his uniform and quite possibly even his baseball gear during his period of enlistment. Military stenciling attributing the foot locker to Musial appears on the lid along with other writing, with addresses both for Musial's base in San Francisco and his home in Donora, Pennsylvania. Dimensions 14x18x34". The foot locker exhibits expected wear but remains solid and complete. A special relic of war-time baseball.
Starting Bid: $250

81440   1945 Stan Musial Owned & Worn Navy Peacoat. A key relic from Musial's admirable service to our nation during the Second World War. This is his Navy peacoat, crafted from heavy wool and twice stenciled with his name at interior lining. No sizing labels inside, but correct for The Man's six foot, 175 pound frame.

Starting Bid: $250

81439   1945-46 Stan Musial US Navy Dress Blues Uniform & Related Ephemera from The Stan Musial Collection. A full St. Louis Cardinals uniform once owned and worn by Musial would have a steep five-figure price tag attached, and a strong argument could be made that this offering is just as significant. Presented is the full Navy dress blues uniform of hat, jacket and pants, each garment identified within as belonging to the legendary slugger. We encourage those bidders reading this text in our printed catalog to visit our online lot listing for images of the various attributions. All garments show wear but are in fine condition and would make an impressive display on a mannequin. Also included within the lot are the following: 1) Large photo of Musial's regiment with The Man fifth from right in the front row (10x16"). 2) Two documents relating to Musial's honorable discharge, one signed by Musial with his fingerprint. 3) Six documents relating to the "Selective Service System" involving Musial's enlistment in 1944. All documents are in strong condition.

Starting Bid: $1,000

81441   1960's Stan Musial Visits Vietnam Photograph Album.
Approximately thirty snapshots from the Hall of Famer's trip to visit the troops during the Vietnam War. At least four picture Musial; the rest presumably find him on the other side of the camera. Some marvelous, previously unseen images of this controversial conflict in Southeast Asia. Photos are in fine condition.

No Minimum Bid

81442   1940 Daytona Beach Islanders Team Signed Baseball with Musial, Dickie Kerr from The Stan Musial Collection. The two recognizable names on this Official Florida State League sphere bring us to this exciting identification, as the 1919 Chicago White Sox pitcher was manager of the Daytona Beach Islanders team that carried a nineteen-year old outfielder named Stan Musial on his roster. Musial and Kerr rate 9/10 and 8/10 respectively, with the balance of the thirteen autographs averaging 7/10. *Pre-certified by PSA/DNA.*
Starting Bid: $200

81444   1940 Daytona Beach Islanders Team Signed Baseball with Musial, Dickie Kerr from The Stan Musial Collection. One of three Islanders baseballs presented within this collection, the earliest Musials on horsehide we've ever encountered. Only two of the names will be familiar to the average baseball historian, those of Musial himself and "Honest Dickie" Kerr, a non-conspiring member of the notorious 1919 Chicago White Sox. Musial and Kerr rate 7/10, with the balance of the fourteen autographs about the same. Ball is an "Official Big League" model. *Pre-certified by PSA/DNA.*
Starting Bid: $200

81443   1940 Daytona Beach Islanders Team Signed Baseball with Musial, Dickie Kerr from The Stan Musial Collection. A nineteen-year old Man in the making rose to the top of the minor league ranks under the tutelage of manager Dickie Kerr, best remembered as a rookie ace southpaw for the 1919 Chicago White Sox. Each appears among the fifteen autographs on this Official Florida State League sphere beneath a vintage coating of shellac, with Musial boldly taking sweet spot honors. Autograph quality averages 6/10 with the notables stronger. *Pre-certified by PSA/DNA.*
Starting Bid: $200

81445   1942 New York Yankees Partial Team Signed Baseball from The Stan Musial Collection. Musial meets the enemy. The Cards took just five games to defeat these American League Champs, and this is Stan's personal keepsake from the vanquished Yanks. Fifteen signatures include Dickey, Hassett, Murphy, Rolfe, Chandler. No DiMaggio, Gordon, Rizzuto. ONL (Giles). Signatures average 7/10. *Pre-certified by PSA/DNA.*
Starting Bid: $150

81446   1942 St. Louis Cardinals Team Reunion Signed Baseball from The Stan Musial Collection. A first taste of World Championship glory for the owner of this high-grade sphere, who completed his sophomore MLB season with a four-to-one Fall Classic thumping of Joe DiMaggio and the New York Yankees. Fifteen members of that team gathered to bask in the good memories at some time during the Warren Giles administration (1951-69), signing this ONL (Giles) sphere for posterity. Along with Musial himself, we find Southworth, Slaughter, Cooper, Crespi, Moore, Gumbert and more. Autographs average 8.5/10 on clean white horsehide. *Pre-certified by PSA/DNA.*

Starting Bid: $250

81448   1944 St. Louis Cardinals Team Signed Baseball from The Stan Musial Collection. The greatest year in St. Louis baseball history, as both pennants and the entirety of Fall Classic play were housed at Sportsman's Park. This is the team that was left standing after six games of World Series action, and twenty-five World Champions have left their mark on this ONL (Frick) orb. Notables include Musial, Schoendienst, Southworth, Wilks, Brecheen, Kurowski, Marion, Cooper, Lanier, Wares and more. Autograph quality averages 8.5/10. Possibly the finest representation extant. *Pre-certified by PSA/DNA.*

Starting Bid: $300

81447   1943 St. Louis Cardinals Team Signed Baseball from The Stan Musial Collection. The Cards won 105 contests to claim the pennant by an eighteen game margin, but fell to the mighty Yanks in five Fall Classic contests. Twenty-three National League Champs congregate on the game used surface of this ONL (Frick) ball, averaging 8.5/10 in strength. Notables: Musial, Southworth, Marion, Brazle, Cooper, Kurowski, Hopp and more. *Pre-certified by PSA/DNA.*

Starting Bid: $200

81449   1944 St. Louis Cardinals Team Signed Baseball from The Stan Musial Collection. For the first time since 1922, when the Giants and Yankees shared the Polo Grounds, the World Series was contested in a single stadium, and presented is a high-grade ONL (Frick) sphere deriving from that all-St. Louis Fall Classic season. Twenty-five World Champions appear in 8/10 and better fountain pen ink on the pristine white horsehide, including Musial himself, Southworth, Brecheen, Wares, Lanier, Marion, Kurowski, Cooper, Hopp and more. Quite possibly the finest representation extant. *Pre-certified by PSA/DNA.*

Starting Bid: $300

81450   1945-46 US Navy Baseball Team Signed Baseball from The Stan Musial Collection. Musial and former Brooklyn Dodgers star Cookie Lavagetto are the only names you'll recognize on this "Official League Ball" with patriotic "US" stamping, but the World War II vintage is the big appeal here. Eighteen autographs average 8/10 beneath a vintage coating of shellac, a special keepsake of The Man's service to our nation during the most significant conflict in world history. *Pre-certified by PSA/DNA.*

Starting Bid: $200

81451   1945-46 US Navy Team Signed Baseball from The Stan Musial Collection. Patriotic sphere dates from The Man's term of service to Uncle Sam, featuring twenty-one autographs including Musial himself and Cardinals teammates Erv Dusak and Whitey Kurowski. Signature quality averages 7/10. Light shellac. *Pre-certified by PSA/DNA.*

Starting Bid: $200

81452   1945-46 US Navy Baseball Partial Team Signed Baseball from The Stan Musial Collection. Another patriotic souvenir of The Man's noble service to our nation's war effort. Musial himself is really the only name on the "Official 97 League" sphere that classifies as a household one, and we note that the "Chuck Klein" signing here is actually Musial's Cardinals teammate Lou Klein and not the Hall of Famer. Fourteen autographs are sealed beneath a vintage coating of shellac at an average 8/10 strength. *Pre-certified by PSA/DNA.*

Starting Bid: $100

81453   1945-46 US Navy Baseball Team Signed Baseball from The Stan Musial Collection. Another team ball from Musial's days of service to the Second World War. Musial himself is absent from the twenty-three signatures that adorn this "Official 97 League" sphere, and Dick Sisler and Ed Miksis are the only names we recognize. Autographs average 8/10 and the ball exhibits scattered staining. *Pre-certified by PSA/DNA.*

Starting Bid: $100

81454   1945-46 US Navy Baseball Team Signed Baseball from The Stan Musial Collection. Part baseball memorabilia, part militaria, the presented sphere was toted back to civilian life by The Man after his brave term of service to the World War II effort was complete. Most of the names of his Navy team-mates will not be familiar, but Musial himself isn't the only Big Leaguer among the twenty-six autographs sealed beneath a vintage coating of shellac on the provided "Official 97 League" horsehide. Other recognizable names include Hall of Famer Billy Herman, Hugh Casey (who would commit suicide in 1951), Herman Franks, Charlie Gilbert, Johnny McCarthy and more. Signatures average 8.5/10. *Pre-certified by PSA/DNA.*

Starting Bid: $250

81456   1946 St. Louis Cardinals Team Signed Baseball from The Stan Musial Collection. Yet another World Championship sphere from the protectors of the Curse of the Bambino. Eighteen autographs from the Sox blockers include Mad Dash artisan Enos Slaughter on the sweet spot, Wares, Kurowski, Rice, Brazle, Brecheen, Sisler and more. No Musial, Schoendienst. *Pre-certified by PSA/DNA.*

Starting Bid: $150

81455   1946 St. Louis Cardinals Team Signed Baseball from The Stan Musial Collection. It's a season best remembered for Enos Slaughter's Mad Dash that sunk the Sox and earned Musial his third and final World Championship ring. This Hall of Fame pair shares space on a side panel of the provided ONL (Frick), joined by twenty-two teammates including Schoendienst, Moore, Marion, Dusak, Kurowski, Brecheen, Brazle and Dyer. *Pre-certified by PSA/DNA.*

Starting Bid: $300

81457   1946 St. Louis Cardinals Team Signed Baseball from The Stan Musial Collection. Enos Slaughter's Mad Dash proved the difference in this sea-son's tense World Series battle with Ted Williams and his Boston Red Sox, and that Hall of Fame speedster shares space on the provided ONL (Frick) sphere with the man who saved it for posterity. Along with Country and The Man, we find twenty-two fellow World Champs, notably Schoendienst, Marion, Garagiola, Burkhart, Pollet, Kurowski, Dusak and newly minted skipper Eddie Dyer. Signatures average a magnificent 8.5/10. Arguably the best '46 Cards ball on Earth when considering condition and former ownership. *Pre-certified by PSA/DNA.*

Starting Bid: $300

81458   1946 St. Louis Cardinals Team Signed Baseball from The Stan Musial Collection. Mad Dasher Enos Slaughter is counted among the twenty-one World Champs that share space on this ONL (Frick) orb, a key relic in the extension of the Curse of the Bambino. The ball's owner Stan Musial is here as well, along with Moore, Sisler, Marion, Kurowski, Gonzales, Brazle and more. Signatures average 7/10. The fourth and final World Series appearance for The Man. *Pre-certified by PSA/DNA.*

Starting Bid: $300

81459   1946 St. Louis Cardinals Team Signed Baseball from The Stan Musial Collection. The World Champs! This is the squad that denied Ted Williams his one chance at Fall Classic glory, twenty-four of them congregated on this ONL (Frick) baseball. Mad Dasher Enos Slaughter is here, as are Musial, Schoendienst, Garagiola, Dyer, Dickson, Marion, Kurowski, Sisler and more. Signature quality averages 8/10. A terrific representation with unbeatable provenance. *Pre-certified by PSA/DNA.*

Starting Bid: $375

81460   1947 St. Louis Cardinals Team Signed Baseball from The Stan Musial Collection. A monumental season in Major League history, the first to reject the long and ugly tradition of racial segregation. The Cards would finish second to Jackie Robinson's Brooklyn Dodgers in the '47 pennant race. Twenty-nine autographs from the runners-up appear on this ONL (Frick) ball at an average strength of 8/10. Notables: Musial, Medwick, Schoendienst, Marion, Dyer, Garagiola, Moore, Dusak, Moore and more. *Pre-certified by PSA/DNA.*

Starting Bid: $200

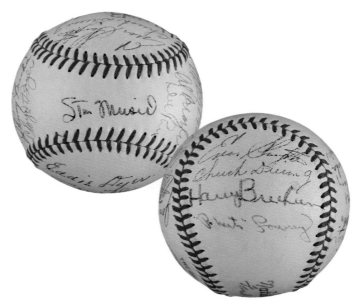

81461   1948 St. Louis Cardinals Team Signed Baseball from The Stan Musial Collection. They outpaced the 1947 National League Champion Brooklyn Dodgers, but couldn't catch the mighty Boston Braves, taking the Senior Circuit silver medal in this '48 pennant race. Stan Musial boldly claims the sweet spot of the provided ONL (Frick) baseball, joined by twenty-one fellow redbirds including Slaughter, Schoendienst, Lanier, Moore, Marion, Brazle, Brecheen, Lowrey and Garagiola, among others. Autograph quality averages a fairly consistent 8/10. *Pre-certified by PSA/DNA.*

Starting Bid: $300

81462   1948 St. Louis Cardinals Partial Team Signed Baseball from The Stan Musial Collection. Gashouse Gangster and 1937 Triple Crown winner Joe Medwick closes out his Hall of Fame career with a perfect sweet spot signature on this ONL (Frick) ball. A dozen signatures are here in total, including Musial himself, Hearn, Wilks, Dickson, Brecheen and Burkhart. Autographs average 9/10. *Pre-certified by PSA/DNA.*
Starting Bid: $200

81464   1954 St. Louis Cardinals Team Signed Baseball from The Stan Musial Collection. Rookie of the Year Wally Moon and veteran legend Stan Musial appear consecutively on a side panel of this nearly pristine ONL (Giles) sphere, perfect for display. Twenty-two autographs are here in total, averaging 9/10. Other notables: Schoendienst, Raschi, Stanky, Repulski, Lowrey, Grammas, Jablonski and more. *Pre-certified by PSA/DNA.*
Starting Bid: $300

81463   1948 St. Louis Cardinals Team Signed Baseball from The Stan Musial Collection. A third and final National League MVP season for Musial, who came up just a single home run short of the Triple Crown in 1948. He properly assumes sweet spot duties on this pristine ONL (Frick) sphere, joined by twenty-two 9+/10 teammates including Schoendienst, Slaughter, Marion, Rice, Brecheen, Jones, Lange and more. A spectacular representation. *Pre-certified by PSA/DNA.*
Starting Bid: $200

81465   1954 St. Louis Cardinals Team Signed Baseball from The Stan Musial Collection. Nearly pristine ONL (Giles) ball features twenty-two members of the 1954 redbirds. Musial is here, of course, along with Schoendienst, Moon, Jablonski, Sarni, Miller, Grammas, Lowrey, Rice, Brazle and more. Likely the finest of its kind on Earth, even without its Musial heritage. *Pre-certified by PSA/DNA.*
Starting Bid: $200

81466 **1956 St. Louis Cardinals Team Signed Baseball from The Stan Musial Collection.** Twenty-four autographs on the provided ONL (Giles) sphere range from light (2/10) to bold (9+/10), with most on the positive side of that range. Notables include Musial, Mizell, Cooper, Dark, Dickson, Hutchinson, Moon and more. Musial's last season near the top of the National League batting average leaderboard before a three-season slump. *Pre-certified by PSA/DNA.*
Starting Bid: $200

81468 **1957 Cincinnati Reds Team Signed Baseball from The Stan Musial Collection.** Other than the fact that the Cards and the Reds share National League affiliation, we aren't certain why this Cincy sphere appears within Musial's collection, but it's a beauty. Twenty-eight autographs average 9/10 on the provided ONL (Giles) sphere, and include Tebbetts, Kluszewski, Post, Bell, Grammas, Lawrence, Burgess, Nuxhall, McMillan and more. *Pre-certified by PSA/DNA.*
Starting Bid: $200

81467 **1957 St. Louis Cardinals Team Signed Baseball from The Stan Musial Collection.** The Cards finished second to a dominant Milwaukee Braves team that would defeat the Yanks in the 1957 Series. But the presented sphere finishes second to none, with twenty-two absolutely flawless blue ink autographs on a snow-white ONL (Giles) model. Notables include Musial, Boyer, Hutchinson, Dark, Smith, Kasko, Moon and more. *Pre-certified by PSA/DNA.*
Starting Bid: $200

81469 **1957 St. Louis Cardinals Team Signed Baseball from The Stan Musial Collection.** Twenty-five signatures appear on this ONL (Giles) sphere saved for posterity by the great Stan Musial, whose number "6" is written on the stamping sweet spot for identification. He appears in signature form as well, along with teammates Wilhelm, Moon, Cooper, Hutchinson, Kasko, Dark, Schofield, Dickson, Mizell and the McDaniel brothers. Signatures average 8/10. *Pre-certified by PSA/DNA.*
Starting Bid: $300

81470　1959 St. Louis Cardinals Team Signed Baseball from The Stan Musial Collection. Blue ink signatures number twenty-nine and average 9/10 in strength on this ONL (Giles) sphere. All your favorite Cards are here: Musial, Gibson, Flood, Boyer, Hemus, Keane, McCarver, Cimoli, Oliver and more. A few stray areas of toning are all that derail a NRMT-MT assessment. *Pre-certified by PSA/DNA.*
Starting Bid: $200

81472　1962 St. Louis Cardinals Team Signed Baseball from The Stan Musial Collection. Yet another nearly pristine sphere from the '62 Cards. Twenty-five autographs include Musial and Keane on the sweet spot, Gibson, Schoendienst, Maxvill, Boyer, McDaniel, Simmons, Oliver and more. ONL (Giles). A splendid relic from The Man's last great season in the Majors. *Pre-certified by PSA/DNA.*
Starting Bid: $200

81471　1961 St. Louis Cardinals Team Signed Baseball from The Stan Musial Collection. Pristine sphere pairs twenty-one bold blue ballpoint autographs with an ivory white ONL (Giles) ball. Notables include Musial, Gibson, Hemus, McCarver, White, Cunningham and Simmons. After posting decidedly un-Musial-like numbers this year, Stan would work hard over the offseason to return for a brilliant 1962 campaign. *Pre-certified by PSA/DNA.*
Starting Bid: $200

81473　1962 St. Louis Cardinals Team Signed Baseball from The Stan Musial Collection. There's a reason you don't see too many '62 Cardinals balls—apparently Stan Musial had them all! Utterly unchanged from its birth over a half century ago, this ONL (Giles) ball features 9+/10 autographs throughout, including Musial, Gibson, Schoendienst, Keane, Boyer, Simmons, Oliver and more. Submit this one for grading! *Pre-certified by PSA/DNA.*
Starting Bid: $300

81474   1962 St. Louis Cardinals Team Signed Baseball from The Stan Musial Collection. Yet another high-grade '62 redbirds sphere from the collection of the franchise's most decorated representative. Musial shares sweet spot duties with manager Johnny Keane, the pair joined by twenty-three teammates including Gibson, Schoendienst, Boyer, Oliver, White, Simmons and Maxvill. Signatures average 8.5/10. ONL (Giles). *Pre-certified by PSA/DNA.*
Starting Bid: $300

81476   1962 St. Louis Cardinals Team Signed Baseball from The Stan Musial Collection. Clearly Musial had a special fondness for this last great season of his career as his collection includes several 1962 team balls. This might be the finest, with 9+/10 signatures on a clean, white ONL (Giles) orb. Twenty-five autographs include Musial, Schoendienst, Gibson, Keane, Simmons, Boyer, McDaniel and more. *Pre-certified by PSA/DNA.*
Starting Bid: $250

81475   1962 St. Louis Cardinals Team Signed Baseball from The Stan Musial Collection. After a three-season slump, Musial roared back to life in 1962, posting a .330 average at the advanced age of forty-one. His memento of that special campaign provides twenty-five autographs, with manager Keane and Musial sharing sweet spot duties. Also present: Gibson, Schoendienst, Boyer, Flood, Simmons, McDaniel, Oliver and more. Autographs average 7/10. *Pre-certified by PSA/DNA.*
Starting Bid: $200

81477   1962 New York City Press Photographers Signed Baseball from The Stan Musial Collection. "To Stan," reads the "Aug. 18, 1962" inscription on the side panel of this ONL (Giles) ball, "From the New York press photographers on your night in the Polo Grounds." *The autographs that adorn the other panels of this ball will be unfamiliar to most, but it's the sentiment that matters here, as it's not every day that a ballplayer is honored on enemy grounds. This auction includes a great photo album from that day at Coogan's Bluff too. Ball's writing averages 6/10. Pre-certified by PSA/DNA.*
Starting Bid: $100

81478   1962 St. Louis Cardinals Team Signed Baseball from The Stan Musial Collection. The Man's last great season. After a lengthy slump, Musial showed there was still some life left in the old man as he led all redbirds with a .330 batting average in 1962. This nearly pristine ONL (Giles) sphere recalls that special campaign. Twenty-five autographs include the sweet spot pairing of Musial and Keane, Gibson, Schoendienst, Boyer, Simmons, McDaniel, Oliver and more. Signatures average 9/10. *Pre-certified by PSA/DNA.*
Starting Bid: $200

81479   1962 St. Louis Cardinals Team Signed Baseball from The Stan Musial Collection. Manager Keane and legend Musial share sweet spot geography on this ONL (Giles) sphere from the last great season of The Man's Hall of Fame career. Other notables include Schoendienst, Gibson, Boyer, Oliver, McDaniel. Twenty-five autographs average 8/10. Ball is ivory white. *Pre-certified by PSA/DNA.*
Starting Bid: $300

81480   1963 St. Louis Cardinals Team Signed Baseball from The Stan Musial Collection. Schoendienst (light), Flood, McCarver, Boyer and Keane are among the notable names on this ONL (Giles) sphere from Musial's final Cards team (though Stan himself is absent). Twenty-two autographs are here in total, with most 8/10 or better but a few that are quite light. *Pre-certified by PSA/DNA.*
Starting Bid: $150

81481   1964 St. Louis Cardinals Team Signed Baseball from The Stan Musial Collection. The first season since World War II that the Cards took the field without Stan Musial, but they took the World Championship anyhow. Twenty-two autographs include Schoendienst, Flood, McCarver, Keane, Simmons, Maxvill, Boyer and more. Most signatures rate 8/10 or better, but a handful are quite light. *Pre-certified by PSA/DNA.*
Starting Bid: $200

81482 **1970's St. Louis Cardinals Old Timers Day Multi-Signed Baseball from The Stan Musial Collection.** Plenty of big names here, but none bigger than the man from whose collection this OAL (MacPhail) baseball derives. Fifteen signatures are here in total, with other notables including Slaughter, Moon, Terry Moore, Mizell, Paul Dean, Harry Walker, Kurowski, Brecheen, Dickson, Carleton and more. Signatures consistently exceed 9/10 in strength. *Pre-certified by PSA/DNA.*
Starting Bid: $100

81484 **1969 Hall of Fame Induction Multi-Signed Baseball from The Stan Musial Collection.** Bob Feller's *"69"* notation suggests this sphere was autographed at the Baseball Hall of Fame on the day of Musial's induction. Surely a particularly special souvenir for The Man, the non-official ball bears seven autographs in total: Feller, Traynor, Hoyt, Stengel, Medwick, Roush and Musial himself. Signatures average 8.5/10. *Pre-certified by PSA/DNA.*
Starting Bid: $300

81483 **Early 1980's St. Louis Cardinals Team Signed Baseballs & One Other from The Stan Musial Collection.** Collection is anchored by three ONL (Feeney) balls each with manager Whitey Herzog on the sweet spot and surrounded by the likes of Ozzie Smith, Keith Hernandez, coach Red Schoendienst and more. Average fifteen signatures per ball, quality 7/10. Finally, we have an Old Timers ball of some sort with signatures from Mize, Musial, Mathews, Feller, Wilhelm, Thomson and more. Autograph quality averages 8/10. Cardinals logo baseball. *Pre-certified by PSA/DNA.*
Starting Bid: $150

81485 **1970's Hall of Famers Multi-Signed Baseball from The Stan Musial Collection.** Nothing but Cooperstown immortals on this OAL (MacPhail) sphere owned by one of the greatest of even this elite brotherhood. Twenty-five autographs are here in total: Grimes, Judy Johnson, Sewell, Dickey, Herman, Banks, Terry, Campanella (clubhouse), Roberts, Spahn, Mathews, Koufax, Cronin, Appling, Kiner, Mize, Travis Jackson, Feller, Musial, Lopez, Irvin, Gehringer, Snider, Averill and Conlan. Some scattered toning, but autographs average 8.5/10. *Pre-certified by PSA/DNA.*
Starting Bid: $300

81486   1981 Hall of Fame Induction Multi-Signed Baseball from The Stan Musial Collection. A small handwritten notation on this OAL (MacPhail) ball dates the signing to 1981, clearly a reference to that year's Cooperstown induction ceremonies due to the cast of characters assembled on its surface. Twenty-three autographs, every one a Hall of Famer: Averill, Wynn, Irvin, Kaline, Feller, Grimes, Conlan, Spahn, Lopez, Sewell, Leonard, Lindstrom (very light), Bell, Gehringer, Judy Johnson, Herman, Dickey, Roberts, Kiner, Mize, Musial, Cronin and Gibson. Unless otherwise noted, autographs average a consistent 9/10. *Pre-certified by PSA/DNA.*

Starting Bid: $300

81488   1980's Hall of Famers Multi-Signed Baseball from The Stan Musial Collection. Nearly pristine sphere was clearly tucked safely away by The Man upon his return from a Cooperstown induction ceremony. Fifteen of his fellow immortals autograph this OAL (Brown) ball in 9+/10 black ink: Doerr, Feller, Wilhelm, Newhouser, Fingers, Lemon, Ford, Kell, Berra, Wynn, Lopez, Killebrew, Hunter, Palmer, Brooks Robinson. *Pre-certified by PSA/DNA.*

Starting Bid: $200

81487   1984 Hall of Fame Induction Ceremony Multi-Signed Baseball from The Stan Musial Collection. Nothing but baseball immortals on this OAL (Brown) sphere saved by The Man as a memento of the 1984 Cooperstown induction ceremony. Twenty-five flawless black ink signatures are here: Kiner, Aparicio, Boudreau, Herman, Killebrew, Conlan, Gehringer, Reese, Sewell, Grimes, Koufax, Leonard, Campanella (wife), Roberts, Judy Johnson, Musial, Irvin, Kell, Wynn, Ferrell, Terry, Drysdale, Mize, Gomez and Kaline. *Pre-certified by PSA/DNA.*

Starting Bid: $300

81489   1986 Hall of Fame Induction Ceremony Signed Baseball from The Stan Musial Collection. Teddy Ballgame and Hap Chandler take sweet spot honors on this OAL (Brown) ball taken home from Cooperstown by Stan Musial after the induction of the 1986 class. Joining Williams and Chandler are eighteen fellow immortals: Doerr, Conlan, McCovey, Gehringer, Slaughter, Sewell, Lemon, Mize, Spahn, Reese, Herman, Judy Johnson, Lopez, Kiner, Gomez, Roberts, Irvin and Musial himself. Signatures average 9/10. *Pre-certified by PSA/DNA.*

Starting Bid: $300

81490   1987 Hall of Fame Induction Ceremony Signed Baseball from The Stan Musial Collection. A jam-packed roster of twenty-five immortals gathered upon this OAL (Brown) sphere at the 1987 Cooperstown induction ceremonies. Musial's personal memento of the event is effectively unchanged from that warm day on the banks of Otsego Lake. The list of signers: Roberts, Gomez, Hunter, Lemon, Dandridge, Billy Williams, Conlan, Kiner, Slaughter, Mize, Reese, Sewell, Boudreau, Dickey, Lopez, Spahn, Chandler, Irvin, Gehringer, Musial, Doerr, Judy Johnson (twice), Banks, Ted Williams and Ferrell. *Pre-certified by PSA/DNA.*
Starting Bid: $300

81492   Circa 1990 Hall of Fame Induction Ceremony Signed Baseball from The Stan Musial Collection. Another keepsake carried home by Musial from the annual Cooperstown induction ceremonies, this one dates to the National League presidency of Bill White (1989-94). Seventeen bold black ballpoint signatures rate 9/10 or better. The roster: Reese, Musial, Stargell, Marichal, Kiner, Schoendienst, Roberts, Billy Williams, Seaver, Irvin, Barlick, McCovey, Snider, Brock, Slaughter, Spahn, Jenkins. Ball is lightly toned and evenly toned. *Pre-certified by PSA/DNA.*
Starting Bid: $300

81491   1988 Hall of Fame Induction Ceremony Signed Baseball from The Stan Musial Collection. An official National League baseball from the presidency of Bart Giamatti serves as the medium for eighteen flawlessly bold autographs of living legends on hand to welcome a new class of Hall of Fame recruits. The roster: Kiner, Lemon, Gehringer, Dandridge, Herman, Roberts, Ted Williams, Musial, Terry, Reese, Kell, Slaughter, Billy Williams, Irvin, Boudreau, Chandler, Gomez and Mize. *Pre-certified by PSA/DNA.*
Starting Bid: $300

81493   1992 Hall of Fame Induction Ceremony Signed Baseball from The Stan Musial Collection. Fourteen autographs on this OAL (Brown) baseball, and each and every signer a Cooperstown immortal. The roster: Doerr, Lemon, Palmer, Kaline, Newhouser, Kell, Wynn, Barlick, Aparicio, Brooks Robinson, Dandridge, Musial, Fingers and Berra. Signatures average 9/10. Ball is clean and white. *Pre-certified by PSA/DNA.*
Starting Bid: $200

81494 **Circa 2000 St. Louis Cardinals Hall of Famers Multi-Signed Baseball from The Stan Musial Collection.** Four legends from the St. Louis birdhouse. Clean, white "Official League" sphere is blessed by the 9/10 and better ink signatures of Musial, Slaughter, Gibson and Brock. *Pre-certified by PSA/DNA.*
Starting Bid: $100

81496 **Circa 1950 Baseball Banquet Multi-Signed Baseball from The Stan Musial Collection.** No apparent theme arises from this collection of signatures, suggesting it was a baseball dinner that served as the genesis. OAL (Harridge) ball is signed by fourteen including Appling, Pesky, Vernon, Keltner, Stirnweiss and more. Autographs average 8/10. *Pre-certified by PSA/DNA.*
Starting Bid: $100

81495 **Circa 2000 St. Louis Cardinals Hall of Famers Multi-Signed Baseball from The Stan Musial Collection.** Four legends from the St. Louis birdhouse. Clean, white "Official League" sphere is blessed by the 9/10 and better ink signatures of Musial, Slaughter, Gibson and Brock. *Pre-certified by PSA/DNA.*
Starting Bid: $100

81497 **1950's Stan Musial, Tris Speaker & Paul Waner Signed Baseball from The Stan Musial Collection.** We aren't certain what event brought this trio of Hall of Fame legends together, but we're glad it happened. It's a high-grade beauty, with a sweet spot Speaker that would command a $20,000 price if the story ended there. Musial appears to the south, and Waner to the west, each in the same 9/10 blue ink. Each is an early member of the illustrious 3,000 Hit Club, the start of a tempting "theme ball" with many more living members to add if desired. The ONL (Giles) ball itself is creamy perfection. The Grey Eagle, The Man and Big Poison, together forever. *Pre-certified by PSA/DNA.*
Starting Bid: $1,000

81498   1950's Tris Speaker, Paul Waner & Stan Musial Signed Baseball. They're numbers four (Musial), five (Speaker) and seventeen (Waner) on the career leader board for Major League hits, responsible for an astounding 10,296 hits between them. We aren't certain what scenario brought this elite sampling of batsmen together, but the ONL (Giles) model sphere places that meeting squarely in Musial's prime, as Giles assumed the National League presidency in 1951, and Speaker passed in 1958. It's the elder statesman who takes sweet spot honors, flanked by Musial to the north and Waner to the south, each at a breathtaking 9/10 level. The ball itself matches the quality of the autographs, presenting a creamy, vintage tone. *Full LOA from PSA/DNA. Auction LOA from James Spence Authentication.*
Starting Bid: $1,000

81500   1980's Mickey Mantle Single Signed Baseballs from The Stan Musial Collection. From one iconic slugger to another. Trio of Mantle singles utilize OAL media—two Browns and a MacPhail—each representation bearing a blue ballpoint sweet spot signature rating 9/10 or better. Some mild toning on two of the balls, but the Musial connection overrides such small concerns. *Pre-certified by PSA/DNA.*
Starting Bid: $150

81499   1980's Old Timers Multi-Signed Baseball from The Stan Musial Collection. Cardinals logo sphere was almost certainly signed at a Busch Stadium Old Timers event, boasting seventeen signatures from former team members and some of their most esteemed opponents. Notable autographs include Musial, Wilhelm, Feller, Mathews, Mize, Oliva, Skowron and Thomson. Signature quality averages 8/10. *Pre-certified by PSA/DNA.*
Starting Bid: $150

81501   1992 Stan Musial, James Michener & Luciano Pavarotti Signed Baseball from The Stan Musial Collection. Two ballplayers, a novelist and an opera singer walked into a bar...and signed this baseball. The punchline may be lacking, but the talent most assuredly is not, as the provided ONL (White) ball is autographed by Musial and his buddies Joe Torre, James Michener and Luciano Pavarotti (who dates his autograph *"92"*). Light toning to the horsehide, but all autographs are 9/10 or better. *Pre-certified by PSA/DNA.*
Starting Bid: $75

81504   Presidents George H.W. & George W. Bush Single Signed Baseballs Lot of 2 from The Stan Musial Collection. Father and son Commanders in Chief appear in this lot built from the voluminous personal collection of the Cardinals' greatest veteran. The elder appears on the sweet spot of an ONL (Coleman) model, while the younger signs a special Presidential ball with the Official Seal of the President, housed in a special display box. Each autograph rates 9/10. *Pre-certified by PSA/DNA.*
Starting Bid: $150

81502   1990's 3,000 Hit Club Signed Baseball from The Stan Musial Collection. It's one of the most exclusive Clubs in the sport, and this high-grade sphere belonged to one of its most esteemed members. Joining Musial on this ONL (Coleman) ball are the following 9+/10 blue ballpoint signatures: Winfield, Rose, Murray, Kaline, Brett, Mays, Molitor, Carew, Aaron, Yastrzemski and Yount. Ball is clean and white. *Pre-certified by PSA/DNA.*
Starting Bid: $200

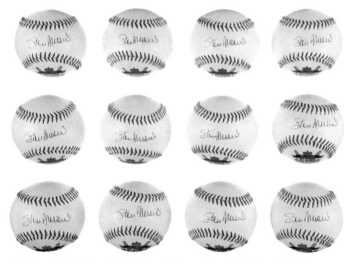

81503   1990's Stan Musial Single Signed Baseball Lot of 12. Stan Musial was the most gracious baseball player of them all. Each of these twelve St. Louis Cardinals Fotoballs is signed across the sweet spot in blue ballpoint by the legendary figure. Most rate 9/10 with the majority being better. *Pre-certified by PSA/DNA.*
Starting Bid: $75

81505   Presidential Single Signed Baseballs Lot of 3 from The Stan Musial Collection. Two Democrats and a Republican from the collection of a true American hero. We begin chronologically with George H.W. Bush, who inscribes his ONL (Coleman) horsehide, *"To Stan—with respect, friendship too!!"* Bill Clinton simply autographs the sweet spot of an ONL (White) ball, while current Commander in Chief Barack Obama likewise provides a sweet spot autograph, on an OML (Selig) model. Autographs average 9/10. *Pre-certified by PSA/DNA.*
Starting Bid: $300

81506   Single Signed Baseballs Lot of 10 from The Stan Musial Collection. Personal horsehide from the collection of one of the sport's most fearsome sluggers. Half of this lot is comprised of pristine Joe Torre singles on OML (Selig) models. Rounding out the balance is a Tony LaRussa, a personalized Don Larsen, a Red Schoendienst (toned), a cleverly inscribed "Greetings to Cardinal Musial from Cardinal Ritter, 1963" and one unknown. All but the unknown signer appear on Official baseballs. Signature quality averages 9/10. *Pre-certified by PSA/DNA.*

Starting Bid: $100

81508   Ted Williams Single Signed Baseballs Lot of 6 from The Stan Musial Collection. Half a dozen singles from The Splendid Splinter. Each autograph rates 9+/10 on the sweet spot of an OAL (Brown) ball, still in the original packaging. Minimal toning is only particularly apparent upon close inspection, otherwise NRMT appearance. Also here are two figural plastic baseball banks with facsimile signatures of the 1940's Cardinals. *Pre-certified by PSA/DNA.*

Starting Bid: $250

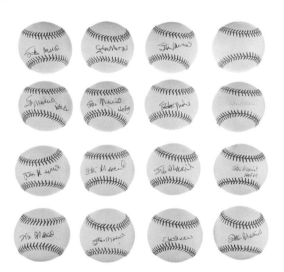

81507   2000's Stan Musial Single Signed Baseball Lot of 16. Stan Musial signed sixteen OML (Selig) baseballs in this collection. Each baseball is signed across the sweet spot. Some of the autographs have mussed slightly. *Pre-certified by PSA/DNA.*

Starting Bid: $100

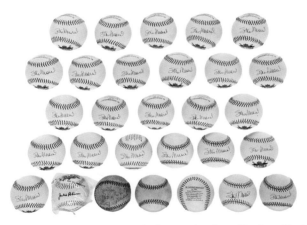

81509   Stan Musial Signed Baseballs Lot of 26 from The Stan Musial Collection. You can never have too much Musial horsehide, and this lot provides a heaping helping of it. We begin with twenty single signed Cardinals logo "Fotoball" models. Next we have three singles on Official models, either National League or World Series. Finally, we have a Musial/Tony Gwynn duo on an ONL (Coleman), a personalized game used ball of indeterminate maker and a Musial single on a 1997 Opening Day stadium give-away ball. Three unsigned balls round out the collection. Signatures average 9/10. *Pre-certified by PSA/DNA.*

Starting Bid: $250

81510 Stan Musial Career Statistics Baseball. Unsigned creation was apparently gifted to the Cardinals great by an admiring fan with a head for statistics and a talent for handwriting. Non-official ball recounts the numerous reasons by Musial was "The Man." Starting Bid: $100

81511 Stan Musial Signed Baseballs Lot of 6. More quality horsehide from the hand of The Man. Two are signed by both Musial and his good buddy, Pulitzer Prize-winning writer James Michener. Three are personalized Musial singles, one of which is a pristine vintage model on an ONL (Giles) sphere. Finally, a red leather unpersonalized single. Autographs average 9/10. *Pre-certified by PSA/DNA.*

Starting Bid: $100

81512 Stan Musial Single Signed "Statistics" Baseballs Lot of 4. The Man lived a long and active life and admittedly signed his share of baseballs during those many decades, but you won't find too many like this. This quartet of ONL (Coleman) spheres begin with a standard *"Stan Musial HOF 69"* sweet spot signature and just keep on going, with the legend's nickname, career stats, MVP seasons and much more penned entirely in his 9+/10 hand. The best Musial singles on Earth, unquestionably. *Pre-certified by PSA/DNA.*

Starting Bid: $100

81513 2000's Stan Musial Single Signed Baseballs Lot of 9. Sweet spot signatures on pristine OML (Selig) spheres. A few are notated with his Hall of Fame induction date. Average quality is 9/10, with a couple dipping a point or two below. *Pre-certified by PSA/DNA.*

Starting Bid: $100

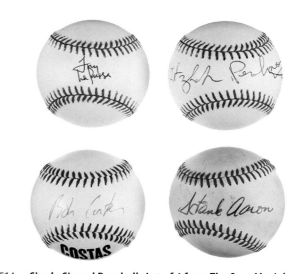

81514 Single Signed Baseballs Lot of 4 from The Stan Musial Collection. A great manager, slugger, conductor and television reporter. A wide array of talents, with elite achievement the common theme. Signers are Tony LaRussa, Hank Aaron, Itzhak Perlman and Bob Costas. Perlman and LaRussa are on Official balls; the others are not. Autograph quality averages 9/10. *Pre-certified by PSA/DNA.*

No Minimum Bid

81516   1943 National League All-Star Team Signed Baseball from The Stan Musial Collection. The tenth anniversary of the Midsummer Classic may have suffered a bit to World War II troop deployment, but the cast of characters on the provided OAL (Harridge) sphere from the Shibe Park contest is still eye-popping. Among the thirty-one signers (of which a percentage appear to be spectators rather than participants) are Frisch, Ott, Lombardi, Herman, Southworth, Musial himself, Owen, Vander Meer, Harry and Dixie Walker, Dahlgren, Vince DiMaggio and many more. Signatures average 8.5/10, and ball is clean and deeply stamped. *Pre-certified by PSA/DNA.*

Starting Bid: $375

81515   1969 George Sosnak Folk Art Baseball Gifted to Stan Musial. If there's a more impressive Sosnak ball out there, we haven't seen it. This former umpire's painstakingly detailed artwork surfaces with some degree of regularity on the auction circuit, but, like Picasso's "Guernica" or Van Gogh's "Starry Night," this is the definitive representation of his brilliance. Practically every statistic of note in the long and distinguished career of The Man is recounted in tiny but perfectly constructed lettering, with a charming portrait of the Cardinals slugger at work filling the scant few square centimeters not packed with text. A masterfully applied clear coat has preserved the integrity of the piece perfectly, without a single scuff or stain to report. Signed *"By Geo. H. Sosnak 1969."* An absolute masterpiece.

Starting Bid: $500

81517   1946 National League All-Star Team Signed Baseball from The Stan Musial Collection. The team was managed by Charlie Grimm, and the result of this Fenway Park exhibition was just that—grim—for this National League team, a twelve to nothing drubbing at the hands of the Americans. Still Musial would have his Boston revenge three months later in the World Series. He is one of nineteen on this ONL (Frick) ball, along with Mize, Schoendienst, Slaughter, Hopp, Kurowski and Grimm. Autographs average 7/10. *Pre-certified by PSA/DNA.*

Starting Bid: $200

81518   1948 National League All-Star Team Signed Baseball from The Stan Musial Collection. Hall of Fame managers Leo Durocher and Bucky Harris represented the National and American Leagues respectively in this Midsummer Classic at Musial's home ballpark. This was the losing side in the five to two Sportsman's Park contest, but the cast of characters represents one of the best teams ever assembled, including Musial, Schoendienst, Ashburn, Mize, Slaughter, Kiner, Durocher and more. Twenty-one signatures appear on the OAL (Harridge) ball, ranging from 4/10 to 8/10. Some ink bleeding and some foxing, but still a solid representation of a rare team ball. *Pre-certified by PSA/DNA.*
Starting Bid: $300

81520   1949 National League All-Star Team Signed Baseball from The Stan Musial Collection. The better of the two '49 All-Star balls presented within this auction, as this model features the full contingent of African-American superstars getting their first taste of Midsummer Classic action: Jackie Robinson, Roy Campanella and Don Newcombe. Twenty-three autographs from that famous Ebbets Field contest appear in total on this ONL (Frick) ball: Slaughter, Spahn, Mize, Kiner, Musial, Hodges, Branca, Seminick, Roe and many more. Autographs average 8.5/10. Certainly one of the finest representations on Earth, even discounting the Musial heritage. *Full LOA from PSA/DNA.*
Starting Bid: $500

81519   1949 National League All-Star Team Signed Baseball from The Stan Musial Collection. Historic Ebbets Field contest was the first to feature African-American players, and one of them—Roy Campanella—is counted among the twenty signatures on this ONL (Frick) ball. Also signing are Musial, Schoendienst, Kiner, Reese, Slaughter, Mize, Spahn, Hodges, Branca, Thomson and more. Autographs average 7/10. *Pre-certified by PSA/DNA.*
Starting Bid: $300

81521   1951 National League All-Star Team Signed Baseball from The Stan Musial Collection. The Nats sailed to an eight to three Midsummer Classic victory on the power of the long ball, putting four into the Briggs Stadium cheap seats, including a fourth inning smash by the owner of this high-grade relic. Musial is joined by twenty-four on this ONL (Giles) sphere, including Spahn, Aaron, Mays, Mathews, Campanella, Roberts, Kluszewski, Friend and more. Signatures average 9/10. Light speckling on ball is little distraction. *Pre-certified by PSA/DNA.*
Starting Bid: $500

81522   1952 National League All-Star Team Signed Baseball from The Stan Musial Collection. A Shibe Park deluge brought the battle to an early conclusion, with this Senior Circuit squad swimming away with the three to two advantage. Twenty-four National Leaguers share space with the ball's owner on this ONL (Giles) orb, including Jackie Robinson, Schoendienst, Irvin, Slaughter, Kiner, Snider, Reese, Durocher, Roberts, Hodges, Thomson and more. Signatures average 8.5/10. *Pre-certified by PSA/DNA.*
Starting Bid: $375

81523   1952 American League All-Star Team Signed Baseball from The Stan Musial Collection. A downpour at Shibe Park brought an end to this Midsummer Classic after five innings, leaving this Junior Circuit crew on the wrong side of a three to two decision. Musial made a point to visit the vanquished Americans and secure this baseball, which is simply bursting with legends. We find Mickey Mantle in his first All-Star appearance sharing space with the ancient Satchel Paige, as well as Fox, Doby, Rizzuto, Stengel, Lemon, Dom DiMaggio, Minoso, Wertz, Avila, McDougald and more. Autograph quality averages 8/10 on the ONL (Giles) sphere. Twenty-five signatures total. *Pre-certified by PSA/DNA.*
Starting Bid: $300

81524   1953 National League All-Star Team Signed Baseball from The Stan Musial Collection. A few stray autographs had us thrown, but the non-All-Stars turned out to be Cincinnati Reds, and this edition of the Midsummer Classic was played at Crosley Field. Discounting those few lesser figures, the talent is jaw-dropping. Future Hall of Famers: Schoendienst, Reese, Roberts, Mathews, Slaughter, Musial, Kiner, Spahn, Ashburn, Jackie Robinson, Campanella, Wilhelm and Snider. Also here are Kluszewski, Hodges, Joe Black and Curt Simmons. Twenty-eight autographs on an ONL (Giles) sphere average 9/10. And it belonged to Stan Musial, who went two for four in the victory over the Junior Circuit! *Pre-certified by PSA/DNA.*
Starting Bid: $300

81525   1953 National League All-Star Team Signed Baseball from The Stan Musial Collection. It was a Crosley Park affair, to which we attribute the appearance of a few stray Reds who didn't make the Midsummer Classic cut. But the bulk of the signers are household names, and include Jackie Robinson, Campanella, Schoendienst, Slaughter, Roberts, Ashburn, Reese, Wilhelm, Snider, Mathews, Hodges, Dressen and more. Twenty-five autographs average 8/10 on an ONL (Giles) sphere. *Pre-certified by PSA/DNA.*
Starting Bid: $300

81526   1953 National League All-Star Team Signed Baseball from The Stan Musial Collection. The Man went two for four in this Crosley Field contest, helping to lead the Senior Circuit to a five to one victory over Casey Stengel's American League squad. Presented is one of Musial's souvenirs from the day, an ONL (Giles) ball autographed by himself and twenty-five of his teammates. These include Jackie Robinson, Campanella, Schoendienst, Roberts, Wilhelm, Ashburn, Mathews, Slaughter, Snider, Reese and more. Signature quality averages 8.5/10. *Pre-certified by PSA/DNA.*

Starting Bid: $375

81527   1955 National League All-Star Team Signed Baseball from The Stan Musial Collection. Many consider it the greatest moment of Musial's career, the National League rallying from a five to nothing deficit to set the stage for his twelfth inning walk-off blast at Milwaukee County Stadium. This is the nearly pristine team ball taken home from the park by the game's hero, signed by thirty members of the unlikely victorious side. Joining Musial in 9/10 or better blue ink are Schoendienst, Snider, Aaron, Mathews, Roberts, Durocher, Banks, Mays, Hodges, Conley, Kluszewski and more. ONL (Giles) ball is lightly and evenly toned to creamy perfection. *Pre-certified by PSA/DNA.*

Starting Bid: $375

81528   1956 American League All-Star Partial Team Signed Baseball from The Stan Musial Collection. The Man went deep in the seventh inning of this Griffith Park victory over the Americans, then visited the opposing dugout to score some signatures. Just a dozen saw fit to fraternize with the enemy, signing at average 8/10 boldness on this OAL (Harridge) sphere. Notables include Fox, Kaline, Wynn, McDougald, Kuenn and Sievers. *Pre-certified by PSA/DNA.*

Starting Bid: $200

81529   1956 National League All-Star Partial Team Signed Baseball from The Stan Musial Collection. Eleven signatures on this OAL (Harridge) ball from the victors in this Griffith Stadium contest. Musial is here twice, joined by Campanella, Snider, Gilliam, Kluszewski, Boyer and more. Signature quality averages 8/10. *Pre-certified by PSA/DNA.*

Starting Bid: $200

81530   1956 National League All-Star Team Signed Baseball from The Stan Musial Collection. Willie Mays and Stan Musial both went yard in the Nats' seven to three defeat of the Americans, and each appear among the twenty-five autographs that fill this ONL (Giles) baseball. Other notables include Campanella, Roberts, Banks, Mathews, Aaron, Spahn, Kluszewski, Boyer and more. Autograph quality averages 8/10. A top-quality representation from one of the game's big heroes. *Pre-certified by PSA/DNA.*
Starting Bid: $300

81532   1957 American League All-Star Team Signed Baseball from The Stan Musial Collection. The Junior Circuit held off a valiant National League surge in the bottom of the ninth to claim victory in this Busch Stadium edition of baseball's most celebrated exhibition. ONL (Giles) ball is autographed by twenty-four at an average strength of 8.5/10. Highlights include Fox, Bunning, Wynn, Kaline, Kell, Berra, Minoso, McDougald, Richardson, Howard, Sievers and more. *Pre-certified by PSA/DNA.*
Starting Bid: $300

81531   1957 American League All-Star Team Signed Baseball from The Stan Musial Collection. Musial's National League team made a brave surge in the bottom of the ninth, but plated only three of the four runs needed to pull even with this crew of Americans in front of his hometown crowd. ONL (Giles) ball from the Busch Stadium contest is autographed by twenty-four including Bunning, Berra, Fox, Wynn, Kell, Kaline, Minoso, Howard, McDougald and more. Autographs average 8.5/10 on the clean, white horsehide. *Pre-certified by PSA/DNA.*
Starting Bid: $300

81533   1957 National League All-Star Team Signed Baseball from The Stan Musial Collection. A three-run bottom of the ninth inning was one run too few to equal the six runs posted by the Americans, leaving Musial's hometown Sportsman's Park crowd briefly thrilled but ultimately disappointed. There's no disappointment in this ONL (Giles) sphere signed by the vanquished All-Stars however, as every autograph rates 9/10 or better. Among the signers: Musial, Spahn (twice), Mathews, Banks, Alston, Burdette, Hodges, Moon and more. Some toning on a couple panels but no loss to autograph boldness. *Pre-certified by PSA/DNA.*
Starting Bid: $300

81534   1958 National League All-Star Team Signed Baseball from The Stan Musial Collection. The Senior Circuit came up a run short to the Americans at Baltimore's Memorial Stadium in the twenty-fifth playing of baseball's most celebrated exhibition. This was perennial All-Star Musial's personal keepsake from the contest, an OAL (Harridge) ball autographed by himself and twenty-three of his teammates. These include Banks, Spahn, Mathews, Mazeroski, Haney, Roseboro, Podres and more. Autographs average 8/10. *Pre-certified by PSA/DNA.*

Starting Bid: $300

81536   Circa 1960 American League Greats Signed Baseball from The Stan Musial Collection. Tons of talent here, but the cast of characters doesn't come close to matching any All-Star roster, so our best guess is this is a souvenir of some form of baseball banquet. The OAL (Cronin) sphere is bursting at the seams with autographs, three dozen in all, and includes the following superstar names: Ted Williams, Mantle, Aparicio, Al Lopez, Brooks Robinson, Ford, Berra, Kaline, Wynn, Fox, Maris, Howard, Minoso and many, many more. Autograph quality averages 8.5/10. *Pre-certified by PSA/DNA.*

Starting Bid: $300

81535   1958 American League All-Star Team Signed Baseball from The Stan Musial Collection. The American League claimed a four to three victory in this twenty-fifth Midsummer Classic, the first in history without an extra base hit. Teddy Ballgame on the sweet spot of this OAL (Harridge) sphere is secretarial, but the other twenty-three are the genuine article and include Mantle, Ford, Berra, Stengel, Wynn, Howard, McDougald and Kuenn. Signatures average 7/10. *Pre-certified by PSA/DNA.*

Starting Bid: $300

81537   1960 National League All-Star Team Signed Baseball from The Stan Musial Collection. Musial pinch hit for Bill Mazeroski in the top of the eighth inning of this Cleveland Municipal Stadium contest, just three months before Maz would club one of the most famous homers in history. Each of these Hall of Fame sluggers is counted among the jam-packed roster of thirty-seven signers. Also here: Clemente, Mays, Banks, Cepeda, Aaron, Alston, Mathews, Friend, Law, Groat, Burgess and many more. Autographs average 8/10 on the OAL (Cronin) medium. *Pre-certified by PSA/DNA.*

Starting Bid: $375

81538   1963 National League All-Star Team Signed Baseball from The Stan Musial Collection. A final Midsummer Classic for the Cardinals great. Musial's souvenir from his twentieth appearance in the game's most heralded exhibition is autographed by a packed roster of thirty-two members of the victorious side at Cleveland Stadium. Musial properly assumes sweet spot honors, joined nearby by the likes of Clemente, Koufax, Drysdale, Mays, Spahn, McCovey, Aaron, Santo, Snider, Cepeda and more. Autograph quality averages a solid 8.5/10. ONL (Giles). *Pre-certified by PSA/DNA.*
Starting Bid: $375

Please note that the lots that follow are not part of The Stan Musial Collection.

81539   1926-2011 St. Louis Cardinals World Series Tickets & Programs Run. Everybody knows that the New York Yankees hold the Major League record for World Series appearances and World Championships, but if you didn't know which team holds the runner-up position, you do now. One dedicated Cards supporter compiled this Fall Classic collection, with a ticket and program from each successful October (unless otherwise noted). All tickets are slabbed "Authentic" by PSA except for 2006 and 2011, which are full tickets graded Mint 9. Programs improve as they get newer, beginning at VG level, to VG-EX in the war years, to EX or better from 1964 forward. Program for 2011 is not present. Years represented: 1926, 1931, 1934, 1942, 1944, 1946, 1964, 1967, 1982, 2006, 2011.
Starting Bid: $500

81540   1948 Stan Musial Game Worn St. Louis Cardinals Jersey—National League MVP Season! It's considered one of the greatest seasons in Major League history, an offensive performance so dominant that Musial didn't just lead the League in ten categories, he *obliterated* it. His 103 extra-base hits was twenty-eight better than the runner-up. Other margins of victory: 429 total bases (113 more), .702 slugging percentage (138 points higher), .376 batting average (42 points higher), 230 hits (40 more), 135 runs (18 more). His 131 runs batted in, forty-six doubles and eighteen triples each led the second-place contender by a half dozen. A single long ball denied him the National League Triple Crown, his career-best thirty-nine one fewer than the forty posted by Hall of Fame sluggers Johnny Mize and Ralph Kiner. The voting for MVP, properly and predictably, was a landslide in The Man's favor.

Presented is one of the most important and desirable post-war jerseys available in the collecting hobby, a creamy home white flannel that thrilled Sportsman's Park throughout this season for the ages. The classic birds and bat logo in its distinctive chenille format adorns the chest, traversing a full-functional zipper and the wide red piping that runs the perimeter of its path and extends to the shoulders and sleeve cuffs. The fabled number "6" remains affixed to verso in red and navy tackle twill, a digit retired from service along with The Man himself on September 29, 1963. Interior collar holds "Rawlings St. Louis" manufacturer's label (worn at upper edge), above a "Dry Clean Only" tag just below. Lower left front tail announces the delectable vintage with "Musial 48" embroidered directly into the jersey body.

Some scattered minor staining, centralized at interior collar and lower ribs, does little to distract the eye and certainly falls well short of diminishing the enormous aesthetic and historical appeal. A Cooperstown-quality relic if there ever was one, this is the definitive game used artifact of Stan the Man. *LOA from MEARS, A8.5. LOA from Heritage Auctions.*

Starting Bid: $10,000

81541   1955 Stan Musial Game Worn St. Louis Cardinals Jersey. *"My feet are killing me,"* American League catcher Yogi Berra complained to Musial as he stepped into the batter's box in the bottom of the twelfth inning of the 1955 All-Star Game. The Cardinals slugger smiled and gave him a wink. *"Relax,"* he ensured Berra, *"I'll have you home in a minute."* He then turned to face Red Sox pitcher Frank Sullivan, blasting his first offering deep beyond the right field wall to keep his promise. The dramatic walk-off shot stands to this day as one of the most commonly retold anecdotes in the Hall of Fame career of Stan "The Man" Musial, who sported this road grey gamer during that memorable 1955 campaign.

The marvelously preserved road grey gamer exhibits solid wear from meetings with the World Champion Brooklyn Dodgers at Ebbets to visits with a rookie Clemente at Forbes Field, the classic chenille birds and bat logo traversing a fully functional zipper front. Red piping rings the cuffs and zipper path, giving way to Musial's retired number "6" in red and navy felt on verso, though we must report this number is restored, the main factor in establishing the MEARS grade. An artfully chain stitched *"Stan Musial"* is sewn directly into the jersey body at lower left front tail, beneath a "Rawlings Hall of Fame Flannel [size] 44" label. Not a single distraction—not a stain or a moth hole—is to be found. Light wear. Musial notates the garment as *"1955 Game Jersey"* beneath his 9+/10 black sharpie signature on lower left chest. *LOA from MEARS, A6. LOA from Heritage Auctions. Full LOA from PSA/DNA (autograph). Full LOA from James Spence Authentication (autograph). COA from Stan Musial (autograph).*

Starting Bid: $7,500

81542 Circa 1956 Stan Musial Game Used First Baseman's Glove. Though he's best remembered as the greatest offensive threat of the National League post-war game, reaching fourth on the career hit list with a staggering 3,630, it shouldn't be forgotten that The Man was no slouch with the leather either, recording 3,730 outs (exactly 100 more than his hit total) in his defensive role. The season of 1956, the probable vintage of the provided first baseman's mitt, was just the second year of Musial's transition from the outfield to the infield, yet his .993 fielding percentage as a first sacker was second only the the Braves' Joe Adcock, besting even the Bums' perennial All-Star Gil Hodges.

"The Glove Collector" newsletter author Joe Phillips provided assistance in the authentication of this rare gear, confirming the professional quality of the "Rawlings TM50" model and the 1955-57 potential range of production, which he further narrows to a likely 1956. A sticker affixed to the glove reads, "Stan Musial 9-25-56," likely applied by the new owner when The Man gifted the well-worn leather four days before the end of the season. Years later the glove was presented to Musial for examination and he confirmed its origin, adding *"My glove"* to his 8/10 blue sharpie autograph.

Leather is quite stiff after years of storage, with minor chipping on back of pocket, but otherwise the glove presents wonderfully and stands as one of just three Musials to reach the hobby's auction block in recent years. *LOA from Joe Phillips.*

Starting Bid: $2,500

81543 Circa 1960 Stan Musial Game Used Bat. The Hillerich & Bradsby M159 was the primary weapon in The Man's arsenal for the final decade of his storied career, the style responsible for his entry into the 3,000 Hit Club and the last of his seven National League batting titles. A quality representation of that important instrument is presented here, perfectly matching the hard-slugging Cardinal's ordering records at thirty-four and a half inches and thirty-one ounces in scale. Ball marks and stitch impressions fill the barrel, where light grain separation speaks to the power that made Musial the most dangerous batter of his day. Ring of tape removed from upper handle. Black sharpie autograph on barrel rates 8/10. *Pre-certified by PSA/DNA.*

Starting Bid: $1,000

81544 1961-63 Stan Musial Game Used Bat. A late-career workhorse from one of the greatest hitters ever to step to into a Major League batter's box, this Hillerich & Bradsby M159 is positively dripping with use, clearly a key instrument in putting the finishing touches on Musial's eye-popping stat line. Leading expert John Taube characterizes the use as *"outstanding,"* drawing attention to the punished grain of the barrel that required nails to tack the heavy checking back into place. Ball marks and stitch impressions are heavily clustered, and cleat marks and green bat rack streaks are clearly apparent. Scoring of the handle is a key Musial trait, and light pine tar remains in this area. Number "6" is written in vintage marker on the knob. Length is thirty-four and a half inches, weight thirty one ounces. *LOA from PSA/DNA. Pre-certified by PSA/DNA (autograph).*

Starting Bid: $2,000

81545 1963 Stan Musial St. Louis Cardinals Player's Contract—His Final Season. History and the collectibles market have always had a soft spot for firsts and lasts, particularly when that which comes in the middle is particularly special. Presented is the closing book end to one of the most special careers in Major League Baseball, the very document that kept a forty-two year old legend in the Cardinals fold for his twenty-second and final campaign. He had signed one of the first $100,000 in National League history five years earlier, but this agreement halved that lofty sum to a figure that felt comfortable to both the team and Musial, who had famously requested a reduction in salary after a disappointing 1959 season.

Certainly The Man's stat line for his last season paled in comparison to those that that earned his baseball immortality, but that's really the point. Few players have exited the game as gracefully as Musial, and his signature on this rather humble contract is a sign of that fact. Most indicative of his importance to the club are addenda stapled to the third page that address bonuses to which Musial is entitled for past performances and language that secures his services as an ambassador for the team for years to come: *"It is understood that effective with calendar year following the calendar year in which the Player retires as and active player, the Club agrees to pay the Player $17,333.33 annually for such public appearances as the Club may request..."*

At the bottom of this page are the signatures of *"Stanley F. Musial,"* National League president Warren Giles and the general manager of the St. Louis Cardinals Vaughan "Bing" Devine. Original storage folds but no other issues of note. *Full LOA from PSA/DNA.*

Starting Bid: $2,500

81546   1979-2003 Stan Musial Jerry Lewis Labor Day Telethon Chairman & Presentation Plates. One of the finest men to grace the baseball diamond, he was no slouch off it either. Presented to Musial in 1979 for his exemplary work with the Jerry Lewis Telethon is this wood award. A gold placard on front indicates Musial was named as "Honorary Telethon Chairman." The award measures 7x9." Also included are two plates (8.25" diameter) honoring the Missouri Athletic Hall of Fame dinner's century of existence. "Homer Laughlin China Pristine" is visible on back.
No Minimum Bid

81548   1967 St. Louis Cardinals Team Signed Baseball. St. Louis was at the top of the baseball landscape in 1967 as they copped a World Series title. Signed by that squad is this ONL (Giles) baseball. The autographs average 6/10 and include the following: Maxvill, Hughes, Jackson, Spiezio, Maris, Johnson, Gagliano, Carlton, Sisler, Flood, Woodall, Briles, Brock, Cepeda, Schoendienst, Bressoud, Hoerner, Tolan and more. *Pre-certified by PSA/DNA.*
Starting Bid: $100

81547   1993 Stan Musial Signed "The Sporting News Stan Musial Scrapbook" Hardcover Books Lot of 6. Offered here is a solid lot of signed hardcover books, each titled "The Sporting News Stan Musial Scrapbook." Signed on each title page by Musial in Mint sharpie, they exhibit perfect condition throughout. *Pre-certified by PSA/DNA.*
No Minimum Bid

81549   1967-68 St. Louis Cardinals Team Signed Baseball. Dating from the two memorable years in which the St. Louis Cardinals made back-to-back World Series, while defeating the Boston Red Sox in the 1967 October Classic, here we present a superbly signed baseball. Exhibiting medium toning and a light application of shellac, it showcases the following keys in ink averaging 5/10 quality: Roger Maris, Steve Carlton, Tim McCarver, Dick Sisler, Lou Brock, Curt Flood, Orlando Cepeda, Red Schoendienst, etc. 28 Signatures are displayed on the ONL (Giles). *Pre-certified by PSA/DNA.*
Starting Bid: $200

81550   1968 St. Louis Cardinals Team Signed Baseball. Curt Flood's mis-judgment of a Jim Northrup liner proved to be the difference in the Cards' fiercely contested seven-game World Series battle with the Detroit Tigers, an instant that haunted the controversial superstar for the rest of his life. His signature joins that of twenty-five fellow National League Champions, including Gibson, Cepeda, Schoendienst, Brock, Carlton, McCarver and Home Run King Roger Maris, who would call it quits at the end of this season. Signature quality averages a consistent 7/10. ONL (Giles). *Pre-certified by PSA/DNA.*

Starting Bid: $300

81552   1972 Hall of Fame Multi Signed Baseball. Undoubtedly this ONL (Feeney) baseball was signed at Cooperstown given the men who all signed are a part of baseball's ultimate team. In all, seventeen legends penned their identity onto the offered orb. A top coating has been added to the baseball, which has "72" written on a side panel. Most of the autographs rate 6/10 to 7/10. Included are: Terry, Musial, Traynor, Berra, Feller, Waner, Frick, Carey, Combs, Wheat, Roush, Hooper, Coveleski, Marquard, Dickey, Grove and Cronin. *Pre-certified by PSA/DNA.*

Starting Bid: $150

81551   1971-82 St. Louis Cardinals Team Signed Baseballs Lot of 4. The St. Louis Cardinals have a connection like few others with their adoring public. Each summer, baseball grabs at the heartstrings of fans. Presented are four team-signed Cardinals baseballs paying tribute to teams of the past. Included are: **1)** 1971 team-signed ONL (Feeney) ball with twenty-two autographs, with an average of 6/10. Included are: Carlton, Zachary, Boyer, Schoendienst, Maxvill, Sizemore, Beauchamp. and more. **2)** 1972 team-signed ONL (Feeney) signed ball with twenty-one. A top coating is applied and most autographs average 7/10. Included are: Boyer, Bare, Schoendienst, Musial, Cruz, Maxvill, Bibby, Brock, Gibson, Sizemore, Simmons and more. **3)** 1973 team-signed ONL (Feeney) ball with twenty-one autographs, most of which are 6/10. Included are signatures of : Schoendienst, Wise, Torre, Sizemore, Brock, McCarver, Gibson, Schultz and more. **4)** 1982 team-signed ONL (Feeney) ball with twenty-two autographs. Most are 6/10 to 7/10. Included are: Herr, Lanier, Sutter, Forsch, Porter, Iorg, Herzog, Schoendienst, Kaat and more. *Pre-certified by PSA/DNA.*

Starting Bid: $150

81553   1970's Collection of Multi Signed Baseballs With Dizzy Dean & Hall of Famers. Offered are three multi-signed baseballs with varying themes. One Hall of Fame baseball was signed at the festivities as Dizzy Dean, Joe Medwick and Stan Musial signed. A comedic twist was added when someone wrote "Marilyn Monroe (alias J.M.) and Musial's wife and Mrs. Babe Ruth signed as well. Eighteen autographs are on the ball, most of family members or partygoers. Batting second is an ONL (Feeney) ball signed by Kiner, Terry, Feller, Musial, Kelly, Waner, Coveleski, Berra, Herman, Cronin and a few more. The autographs average 6/10 to 7/10 and shellac has been added. The final item is a signed ONL (Feeney) ball signed by Musial wishing someone a Happy Birthday, however, Stan the Man did not write the salutation. *Pre-certified by PSA/DNA.*

Starting Bid: $100

81554 **1977 Baseball Greats Multi Signed Baseball.** The overwhelming majority of autographs on this ONL (Feeney) baseball are Hall of Famers of the highest order. Signed by eighteen baseball greats is this fine orb. Signatures include: Waner, Feller, Kiner, Ford, Berra, Herman, Kelly, Terry, Musial, Conlan, Mantle, Marquard, Leonard, Roush, Averill, Coveleski and two more. *Pre-certified by PSA/DNA.*
Starting Bid: $100

81556 **1985-99 Collection of Signed Baseballs Lot of 6.** Presented in this listing are six signed baseballs. Included are: Boggs signed ball with 3000 hit notation, Musial (smeared), Bob Uecker, Leroy Neiman multi signed ball (personalized), Musial multi-signed ball and one more. *Pre-certified by PSA/DNA.*
No Minimum Bid

81555 **1980's Baseball Greats Multi Signed Baseballs Lot of 2.** All but one of the men who have signed baseballs in this listing are in Cooperstown. One St. Louis Cardinals baseball is signed by Mantle, Musial, Ford, Kiner, Conlan, Mays and an unknown name. The ballpoint pennings average 9/10. A second ONL (Feeney) baseball is signed by Lopez, Kell, Musial, Alston, Leonard, Irvin and Roush. "St. Petersburg 3-83" is written on an adjacent side panel. The signatures average 8/10. *Pre-certified by PSA/DNA.*
Starting Bid: $100

81557 **1970's Baseball Greats Multi Signed Baseballs Lot of 2.** Presented are two multi-signed baseballs honoring stars of the past, mostly Hall of Famers. Taking top honors is a multi-signed Baseball Hall of Fame ball decorated with five autographs. Most are 8/10 and include: Dean, Hoyt, Musial, Medwick and one more. The second orb (toned) is signed by Ford, DiMaggio, Kaat and two more. *Pre-certified by PSA/DNA.*
Starting Bid: $150

81558   Stan Musial Single Signed Baseballs Lot of 6. Offered here is a lot of six single-signed baseballs, each featuring Cardinals legend Stan Musial. Presenting sweet spot signatures averaging Mint quality ball-point ink, the OML (Selig - National Baseball HOF commemorative) balls display superbly. *Pre-certified by PSA/DNA.*

No Minimum Bid

81560   Stan Musial Single Signed Baseballs Lot of 12. Offered here is a lot of 12 single-signed baseballs, each featuring Cardinals legend Stan Musial. Presenting sweet spot and side panel signatures averaging NM quality ball-point ink, the lot includes six OML (Selig) balls and six OML (Selig - 2009 A.S. Game) balls. Leather ranges from no toning to light traces of toning throughout. *Pre-certified by PSA/DNA.*

Starting Bid: $100

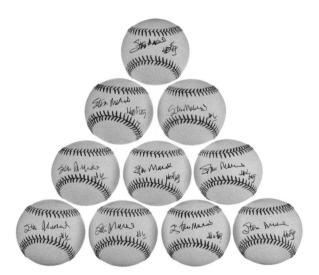

81559   Stan Musial Single Signed Baseballs Lot of 10. Offered here is a lot of 10 single-signed baseballs, each featuring Cardinals legend Stan Musial. Presenting sweet spot signatures averaging Mint quality ball-point ink, the OML (Selig) balls include four with "#6" inscribed and six with "HOF 69" in the pen of the great Hall of Famer. *Pre-certified by PSA/DNA.*

Starting Bid: $100

81561   Stan Musial Signed Cardboard Strips Lot of 30. Offered here is a pair of uncut heavy cardboard sheets, each featuring 15 signatures from Cardinals legend Stan Musial. Presenting 30 Mint ink exemplars in all, each sheet measures at a total of 3.25x13.5" (1x3.25" strips). *Pre-certified by PSA/DNA.*

No Minimum Bid

81562 Stan Musial Signed Holographic Stickers Lot of 180. Offered here is a lot of 180 holographic stickers, each signed by Cardinals legend Stan Musial. Averaging Mint signatures throughout, the .5x2" strips are still affixed to their original sheets and never used. *Pre-certified by PSA/DNA.*
Starting Bid: $150

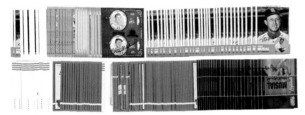

81563 Stan Musial Signed Cards Lot of 189. Offered here is an investment lot of 189 signed cards, each featuring Cardinals legend Stan Musial. Averaging NM-MT quality throughout, each showcases a Mint signature from the Hall of Famer, and the lot includes examples from the following issues: Topps Heritage, Donruss Team Heroes, Diamond Kings, Donruss Classics, Fleer, Topps and Donruss Americana. *Pre-certified by PSA/DNA.*
Starting Bid: $150

81564 Stan Musial Signed St. Louis Cardinals Caps and Telegram Prints Lot of 12. Offered here is a nice lot of signed pieces, each featuring St. Louis Cardinals legend Stan Musial. Included are six "New Era [size] 7.5" wool Cardinals caps and six 4.5x6.5" replica prints of a telegram from Rogers Hornsby congratulating Musial on tying his record as National League batting champion. Mint signatures are displayed throughout. *Pre-certified by PSA/DNA.*
Starting Bid: $100

81565 Stan Musial Signed Oversized Photographs and Magazines Lot of 18. Offered here is a nice lot of 18 pieces of memorabilia, each signed by Cardinals legend Stan Musial. Included are the following: six 11x14" black and white photographs; six 11x14" color prints; six August 2-9, 2010 "Sports Illustrated" magazines. Each piece presents Mint quality sharpie. *Pre-certified by PSA/DNA.*
Starting Bid: $100

81566 Circa 2000 Stan Musial Signed Hand Print. Black ink hand print was applied to a 10x13" sheet of blank charity in support of "Helping Hands" charity, then signed by The Man in 9/10 red sharpie below. See how you measure up to one of the greatest hitters of all time. Hand print is framed to 13x16". *Full LOA from PSA/DNA.*
Starting Bid: $200

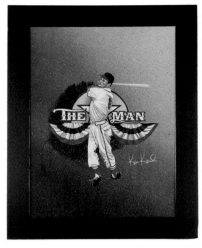

81567   **Circa 2010 Stan Musial Original Artwork by Ken Karl.** Another marvelous study of the Cardinals legend from the mind and brushes of noted Ken Karl, who captures the swing that carried the Cardinals star to the upper reaches of the sport's pantheon. The acrylic on artist's board work measures 17x23" and is matted to final dimensions of 22x28". Fine condition.
Starting Bid: $500

81568   **Circa 2010 Stan Musial Original Artwork by Ken Karl.** Masterful portrait of The Man in his prime is the work of noted Ken Karl, who captures the swing that carried the Cardinals star to the upper reaches of the sport's pantheon. The acrylic on artist's board work measures 17x23" and is matted to final dimensions of 22x28". Fine condition.
Starting Bid: $500

Session Two Lots 81569–82655
Continued in the Sports Memorabilia Catalog

SESSION THREE – THE STAN MUSIAL COLLECTION

Mail, Fax, Internet & Extended Bidding Only Auction #7085
Saturday, November 9, 2013 | 10:00 PM CT | Dallas | Lots 82739–82983

Session Three Lots 82656–82738 and 82984–83526 are found in the Sports Memorabilia Catalog

A 19.5% Buyer's Premium ($14 minimum) Will Be Added To All Lots
To view full descriptions, enlargeable images and bid online, visit HA.com/7085

82739 1953-2009 Stan Musial Collection of Signed Books Lot of 15.

82742 1980-97 Stan Musial Personal Collection of Author Signed Books Lot of 9.

82746 1990 Stan Musial Signed Pilgrimage Book Lot of Six.

82749 Author Signed Book Collection Each Personalized to Stan Musial.

82752 Stan Musial's Personal Library with Twelve Books, Most Inscribed to Him.

82740 1960-90 Collection of Twenty-Two Books From The Stan Musial Collection.

82747 2002-09 Stan Musial Personal Collection of Baseball Books Lot of 13.

82743 1973-2003 Stan Musial Collection of Author Signed Books Lot of 13.

82750 Stan Musial Personal Author Signed Books Lot of 25.

82753 1980's Ernie Banks Inscribed Photograph from The Stan Musial Collection.

82741 1960's Stan Musial Signed Magazine Lot of 20.

82744 1980's-2000's Stan Musial & Other Authors Signed Books Lot of 21.

82748 Hall of Fame Sportswriter Bob Broeg Inscribed & Signed Books Lot of 17 from The Stan Musial Collection.

82751 Stan Musial Personally Owned Books Lot of 14, Most Signed and Inscribed.

82754 Early 1990's Tony Gwynn Signed Photograph to Stan Musial.

82745 1990 Stan Musial Signed Pilgrimage Book Lot of Six.

82755 1990's Stan Musial & Tony Gwynn Signed Magazine Cover.

82756 Early 1990's Tony Gwynn Signed Photograph to Stan Musial.

82757 1994-2012 Stan Musial Collection of Hall of Fame Photos Lot of 14.

82758 1996 Louisville Slugger Museum Multi Signed Photo From Stan Musial Collection.

82759 1990's Stan Musial Personal Photos, Painting & Signed Brochures.

82760 Stan Musial Signed Large Photographs Lot of 24 from The Stan Musial Collection.

82761 Stan Musial Signed Large Photographs Lot of 12 from The Stan Musial Collection.

82762 2007 Stan Musial & Ryan Howard Signed Large Photographs from The Stan Musial Collection.

82763 Stan Musial Personal Collection of Signed Oversized Photographs Lot of 7 With Warren Buffett.

82764 2000's George W. Bush Autopen Signed Photograph from The Stan Musial Collection.

82765 2000's Stan Musial Signed Large Photographs Lot of 5.

82766 Stan Musial Signed Large Photographs Lot of 3 from The Stan Musial Collection.

82767 Stan Musial Signed Photocopies Lot of 36 from The Stan Musial Collection.

82768 Signed Photographs and Original Art from The Stan Musial Collection.

82769 Autographed Images Lot of 28 from The Stan Musial Collection.

82770 Stan Musial Signed Photographs, Magazines and More Lot of 33.

82771 Stan Musial Personal Photos Lot of 66 - Some Signed.

82772 1978 Cardinals & Anheuser Busch Commemorative Print Lot of 76.

82773 1986 Stan Musial Statistics Displays Lot of 6.

82774 Stan Musial Signed Prints Lot of 250+ from The Stan Musial Collection.

82775 St. Louis Cardinals Legends Multi-Signed Large Prints Lot of 12 from The Stan Musial Collection.

82776 Posters & Various Ephemera from The Stan Musial Collection.

82777 Stan Musial Signed Posters Lot of 23 from The Stan Musial Collection.

82778 1988 Stan Musial, Eddie Mathews & Bob Feller Signed Prints Lot of 7 from The Stan Musial Collection.

82779 Posters, Photographs & Proclamations from The Stan Musial Collection.

82780 1998-09 Stan Musial Signed Posters & Photos Lot of 8.

82781 Stan Musial Signed Posters & Photographs Lot of 50+.

82782   1980's 3,000 Hit Club Signed Posters Lot of 11.

82783   2009 Stan Musial & Albert Pujols Signed Posters Lot of 3.

82784   Stan Musial Signed Vintage Photographs Lot of 5 from The Stan Musial Collection.

82785   1958 Stan Musial & Warren Spahn Signed Photographs Lot of 4 from The Stan Musial Collection.

82786   Stan Musial Original Photographs Lot of 53.

82787   Stan Musial Original Photographs Lot of 46.

82788   Stan Musial Original Photographs Lot of 26.

82789   Stan Musial Signed Original Photographs Lot of 35.

82790   Stan Musial Original Photographs Lot of 35.

82791   Stan Musial Original Photographs Lot of 22.

82792   Stan Musial Signed Original Photographs Lot of 27.

82793   Stan Musial Signed Original Photographs Lot of 38.

82794   Stan Musial Signed Original Photographs Lot of 20.

82795   Stan Musial Signed Original Photographs Lot of 36.

82796   Stan Musial Signed Original Press Photographs Lot of 24.

82797   Stan Musial Signed Original Photographs Lot of 23.

82798   Stan Musial Signed Photographs Lot of 36.

82799   Stan Musial Signed Original Photographs Lot of 31.

82800   Stan Musial Signed Original Press Photographs Lot of 28.

82801   Stan Musial Signed Original Press Photographs Lot of 21.

82802   Stan Musial Signed Original Photographs Lot of 25.

82803   Stan Musial Signed Contemporary Photographs Lot of 31.

82804   Stan Musial Signed Original Photographs, Prints, Etc. Lot of 28.

82805   Stan Musial Signed Original Photographs and Advertisements Lot of 16.

82806   Stan Musial Signed Original Photographs and Prints Lot of 22.

82807   Stan Musial Signed Original Photographs, Prints, Etc. Lot of 27.

82808   Stan Musial Signed Photographs, Clippings, Etc. Lot of 20.

82809 Stan Musial Signed Original Oversized Photographs Lot of 16.

82810 Stan Musial Signed Original Press Photographs Lot of 25.

82811 Stan Musial Signed Original Press Photographs and Prints Lot of 25.

82812 Stan Musial Signed Original Press Photographs Lot of 32.

82813 Stan Musial Signed Original Press Photographs Lot of 13.

82814 1950's Stan Musial & Biggies Restaurant Mirror & Signed Photo.

82815 1963 Stan Musial Retirement Lot with Autographs from The Stan Musial Collection.

82816 Collection of Stan Musial Signed Programs & Tickets - Including First Issue of Sports Illustrated.

82817 Signed and Unsigned Record Albums & More from The Stan Musial Collection.

82818 Stan Musial Signed Tickets & Index Cards—Over 100 Autographs!

82819 Birthday & Get Well Cards Sent to Stan Musial.

82820 1980's-90's Stan Musial & Others Signed Cards Lot of 100+.

82821 2000's Stan Musial Signed Checks Lot of 12.

82822 Stan Musial Signed Receipts Lot of 20+.

82823 Stan Musial Signed Street Signs Lot of 2.

82824 Ted Williams Signed Prints Lot of 10 from The Stan Musial Collection.

82825 Ted Williams Signed Prints Lot of 10 from The Stan Musial Collection.

82826 Ted Williams Signed Prints Lot of 10 from The Stan Musial Collection.

82827 Ted Williams Signed Photographic Prints Lot of 10 from The Stan Musial Collection.

82828 Ted Williams Signed Prints Lot of 10 from The Stan Musial Collection.

82829 Ted Williams Signed Prints Lot of 10 from The Stan Musial Collection.

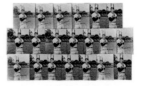

82830 Ted Williams Signed Photographic Prints Lot of 10 from The Stan Musial Collection.

82831 Ted Williams Signed Prints Lot of 10 from The Stan Musial Collection.

82832 Ted Williams Signed Photographic Prints Lot of 10 from The Stan Musial Collection.

82833 Ted Williams Signed Prints Lot of 10 from The Stan Musial Collection.

82834 Ted Williams Signed Prints Lot of 10 from The Stan Musial Collection.

82835 Ted Williams Signed Photographs Lot of 20 from The Stan Musial Collection.

82836 1970's-90's Stan Musial Owned Mini Bats (20) & Retail Model Gloves (2).

82837 Stan Musial Owned Baseball Bats (6) & Baseballs (3).

82838 3,000 Hit Club Multi-Signed Bat.

82839 Stan Musial Bats Lot of Eleven with Six Signed Examples.

82840 Stan Musial Signed Bats Lot of 6.

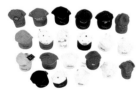

82841 2008 Hall of Fame Induction Multi-Signed Bat.

82842 Stan Musial Signed & Unsigned Baseball Caps Lot of 27.

82843 Stan Musial Retail Model Gloves (5) and Cardinal Cap with Two Autographs.

82844 Stan Musial Signed & Unsigned Ephemera Collection.

82845 Stan Musial Signed "The Legend Lives" Pewter Statues Lot of 3.

82846 Stan Musial Signed Figures and Plates.

82847 Stan Musial Oversized Display Pieces Lot of 7.

82848 1992 Stan Musial Personal Gartlan Statue From Personal Collection Artist's Proof.

6

82849 Stan Musial Retired Number "6" Flag Flown at Busch Stadium.

82850 Stan Musial Presentational Box from the San Diego Padres & More.

82851 1995-2007 Stan Musial Personal Collection of Hall of Fame Invitations & Pins.

82852 Stan Musial Wooden Baseball Case, Bat Racks (2) & Statue.

82853 Stan Musial Used Personalized Binders Lot of 6.

82854 Stan Musial Season Passes & Schedules Lot of 15.

82855 Stan Musial Owned Jewelry & Related Items.

82856 Stan Musial Personally Owned Lapel Pins Lot of 24.

82857 Stan Musial Hall of Fame Pins Lot of 8.

82858 Stan Musial Assortment of Pins, Presentational Wristwatches, Etc.

82859 2004 Stan Musial Legends of the Park Bobblehead Lot of 20 & More.

82860 Scrapbook of Fan Letters & Various Ephemera from The Stan Musial Collection.

82861 Author Inscribed & Signed Books Lot of 24 from The Stan Musial Collection.

82862 Unsigned Books from The Stan Musial Collection.

82863 Stan Musial Personally Owned Books Lot of 22.

82864 Author Signed Books Lot of 11 from The Stan Musial Collection.

82865 1930's-90's Miscellaneous Stan Musial Collectibles Incl. Prayer Book & HOF Issued Items.

82866 1980's Perez-Steele Unsigned Cards from The Stan Musial Collection.

82867 Stan Musial Personally Owned Baseball Books Lot of 19.

82868 Author Signed Books to Stan Musial Lot of 17.

82869 Assortment of Stan Musial Publications With Sportsman of the Year Leatherbound Gift.

82870 Stan Musial Assorted Book Lot.

82871 1940's-50's Stan Musial Scrapbooks Lot of 4.

82872 1940's-50's Stan Musial Scrapbooks Lot of 5.

82873 Stan Musial Personal Bibles (2) and Other Religious Ephemera.

82874 Early 1940's Stan Musial Personal Scrapbooks Lot of 4.

82875 Stan Musial Ephemera Lot with Books, Playing Cards.

82876 1941 Stan Musial Daytona Beach Scrapbook.

82877 Stan Musial Books, VHS Tapes & CD Collection with Some Autographs.

82878 1998-2012 Baseball Hall of Fame Induction Golf Shirts Lot of 7.

82879 Stan Musial Worn Sashes Lot of 4.

82880 Stan Musial Various Collectibles.

82881 Stan Musial Owned & Worn Belt Buckles Lot of 8.

82882 Stan Musial Worn Sweaters Lot of 5.

82883 Stan Musial Worn Garments Lot of 6.

82884 Stan Musial Assorted Clothing Lot of 5.

82885 Stan Musial Hunting/Shooting Clothing Collection.

82886 Stan Musial Formal Wear Collection.

82887 Circa 1980 Stan Musial Owned & Worn Pants Lot of 5.

82888   1980's Stan Musial Blazer and Five Pairs of Pants.

82889   Stan Musial Worn Garments Lot of 5.

82890   Circa 1990 Stan Musial Worn Dress Shirts Lot of 10.

82891   Stan Musial Owned & Worn Pants (5) & Blazer.

82892   Stan Musial Owned & Worn Pants Lot of 5.

82893   Stan Musial Owned & Worn Suit & Pants (6 pairs).

82894   2000's St. Louis Cardinals Jackets Worn by Stan Musial.

82895   Stan Musial Worn Garments Lot of 10.

82896   1990's Stan Musial Owned & Worn Clothing.

82897   Stan Musial Owned & Worn Garments Lot of 12.

82898   Stan Musial Owned & Worn Clothing Lot.

82899   Circa 1990 Stan Musial Worn Dress Shirts with Neckties & More.

82900   Stan Musial Owned & Worn Neckties Lot of 10.

82901   Stan Musial Owned & Worn Neckties Lot of 10.

82902   Stan Musial Owned & Worn Neckties Lot of 10.

82903   Stan Musial Owned & Worn Neckties Lot of 5.

82904   Stan Musial Owned & Worn Neckties Lot of 5.

82905   Stan Musial Old Timers Game Worn Socks & Stirrups.

82906   Circa 1990 Stan Musial Worn Dress Shirts Lot of 4.

82907   Circa 1990 Stan Musial Worn Dress Shirts Lot of 4.

82908   Stan Musial Golf Bag/ Luggage Tags, Harmonicas & Business Cards.

82909   Stan Musial Golf Bag Cover.

82910   Stan Musial Pool Cues Lot of 4 & Bat Rack.

82911   Stan Musial Golf Clubs Lot of 4.

82912   Stan Musial Personally Owned Harmonicas (19) & Money Clips (15).

82913   Stan Musial's Personal Gun Rack from The Stan Musial Collection.

82914 **Personally Owned VHS Tapes & Compact Discs from The Stan Musial Collection.**

82915 **1960's Stan Musial Tour of Japan Personal Items and Mementos.**

82916 **Stan Musial Presentational Pens, Pocket Knife & More.**

82917 **Stan Musial Owned Wallets & Various Ephemera.**

82918 **Stan Musial Owned Ephemera including** *"This is Your Life"* **Television Transcript.**

82919 **1969 Stan Musial's Tour of Japan Presentational Wall Calendar.**

82920 **Stan Musial Collection of Pins.**

82921 **Stan Musial Family Crest, "Sports Legend Award" and Desk Clock.**

82922 **Stan Musial Hunting Artifacts.**

82923 **Stan Musial Lot of Personal Mementos.**

82924 **1990's Assortment of Stan Musial Signed Clocks & Other Memorabilia.**

82925 **Contents of Stan Musial's Personal Desk.**

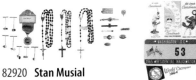

82926 **Stan Musial Signed Presidential Inauguration License Plates & More.**

82927 **Stan Musial Religious Material Including Papal Visit to St. Louis Souvenirs.**

82928 **Stan Musial Souvenir Bricks Lot of 2.**

82929 **Stan Musial Contents of His Personal Desk.**

82930 **1940's-2000's Collection of Stan Musial Personal Photos & Newspaper Photos.**

82931 **Late 1950's Stan Musial Key to the City of Maui and St. Louis Cardinals Pillow.**

82932 **1960's Stan Musial Personal Tickets, Programs & Mementos.**

82933 **1960's Stan Musial Hartland Statues Lot of 5.**

82934 **1965 Stan Musial Presentational Hawaiian Bowl & Plate.**

82935 **1973-96 Stan Musial Personal Items.**

82936 **1973 Presentational Television & Two Blankets from The Stan Musial Collection.**

82937 **1980's Stan Musial Polish Ephemera Lot with Autographs.**

82938 **1986-2007 Stan Musial Presentational Statues Lot of 2.**

82939 **1995 Liberty Bell Cast Iron Replica from The Stan Musial Collection.**

82940 **1996 Topps Legends of the Fifties Bronze Trading Cards Collection.**

82941   2011 "Stan the Man" Musial Life Preserver.

82946   Stan Musial Owned Pocket Knives, Cufflinks, Lighters, Etc.

82951   Stan Musial Framed Memorabilia Lot of 6.

82957   Personally Owned Original Artwork from The Stan Musial Collection.

82962   1960's Stan Musial Signed Personal Photos From Alfred Fleishman.

82942   Stan Musial Personally Owned Cigarette Lighters (14) & Harmonica.

82947   Stan Musial Jewelry Collection with Cardinals Presentational Wristwatch.

82952   Stan Musial Framed Memorabilia Lot of 6.

82958   Personally Received Holiday Cards from The Stan Musial Collection.

82963   Stan Musial Copies of Signed and Unsigned Vintage Photography Lot.

82943   Stan Musial's Jewelry Box with Contents.

82948   Photograph Albums, Luggage, Original Cartoon Art & More from The Stan Musial Collection.

82953   Stan Musial Personally Owned Photography Lot of 11.

82959   Original Artwork & Prints from The Stan Musial Collection.

82964   1940's-60's Stan Musial Personally Owned Large Photographs Lot of 28.

82944   1950-60 Stan Musial Lighter Lot of 20.

82949   Stan Musial Personally Owned Display Pieces Lot of 6.

82954   Stan Musial Signed & Unsigned Framed Memorabilia Lot of 4.

82960   Stan Musial Large Photographs & Newspaper Mock-Ups from The Stan Musial Collection.

82965   1963-67 Stan Musial Photograph Albums Lot of 3.

82945   1950-60 Stan Musial Lighter Lot of 21.

82950   Framed Display Pieces Lot of 5 from The Stan Musial Collection.

82955   1999 Stan Musial Original Artwork.

82956   Stan Musial Framed Memorabilia (with Autographs) Lot of 7.

82961   Personally Owned Posters & Large Photograph from The Stan Musial Collection.

82966   1962 "New York City Honors Stan 'The Man' Musial" Photograph Album.

82967 Stan Musial Photographs Lot of Approximately 100.

82970 1968 St. Louis Cardinals Tour of Japan Photograph Album Belonging to Stan Musial.

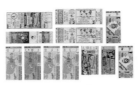

82977 1964-2006 Stan Musial Personal World Series Ticket Lot of 52.

82981 1940's-50's St. Louis Cardinals Uniform/Jacket Patches.

82968 1950's Stan Musial European Vacation Photograph Album.

82971 1958 Stan Musial Personal Tour of Japan Photo Album.

82974 1976-92 Churchill Downs Ticket Stub & Betting Slips Collection from The Stan Musial Collection.

82975 1974-91 Super Bowl Tickets Lot of 21 From Stan Musial Collection.

82978 1990's-2000's Stan Musial Hall of Fame Induction Badges & Season Passes.

82982 Circa 1950 Stan Musial Game Worn Stirrups.

82969 1948-69 Stan Musial Photo Album & Scrapbook Lot of 2.

82972 Stan Musial Original Hunting Photographs Lot of 22.

82976 1980's-2010's St. Louis Cardinals Full Tickets (approx. 100) from The Stan Musial Collection.

82979 Circa 1950 Stan Musial Suitcase.

82983 1968 Stan Musial Statue Unveiling at Busch Stadium Photograph Album.

82973 Stan Musial Original Golf Photographs Lot of 34.

82980 1970's Stan Musial Suitcases Lot of 3.

**Session Three Lots 82656–82738 and 82984–83526
are found in the Sports Memorabilia Catalog**

Terms and Conditions of Auction

Auctioneer and Auction:

1. This Auction is presented by Heritage Auctions, a d/b/a/ of Heritage Auctioneers & Galleries, Inc., or Heritage Auctions, Inc., or Heritage Numismatic Auctions, Inc., or Heritage Vintage Sports Auctions, Inc., or Currency Auctions of America, Inc., as identified with the applicable licensing information on the title page of the catalog or on the HA.com Internet site (the "Auctioneer"). The Auction is conducted under these Terms and Conditions of Auction and applicable state and local law. Announcements and corrections from the podium and those made through the Terms and Conditions of Auctions appearing on the Internet at HA.com supersede those in the printed catalog.

Buyer's Premium:

2. All bids are subject to a Buyer's Premium which is in addition to the placed successful bid:
- Seventeen and one-half percent (17.5%) on Currency, US Coin, and World & Ancient Coin Auction lots, except for Gallery Auction lots as noted below;
- Nineteen and one-half percent (19.5%) on Comic, Movie Poster, Sports Collectibles, and Gallery Auction (sealed bid auctions of mostly bulk numismatic material) lots;
- Twenty-two percent (22%) on Wine Auction lots;
- For lots in all other categories not listed above, twenty-five percent (25%) on the first $100,000 (minimum $14), twenty percent (20%) of any amount between $100,000 and $1,000,000, and twelve percent (12%) of any amount over $1,000,000.

Auction Venues:

3. The following Auctions are conducted solely on the Internet: Heritage Weekly Internet Auctions (Coin, Currency, Comics, Rare Books, Jewelry & Watches, Guitars & Musical Instruments, and Vintage Movie Posters); Heritage Monthly Internet Auctions (Sports, World Coins and Rare Wine). Signature® Auctions and Grand Format Auctions accept bids from the Internet, telephone, fax, or mail first, followed by a floor bidding session; HeritageLive! and real- time telephone bidding are available to registered clients during these auctions.

Bidders:

4. Any person participating or registering for the Auction agrees to be bound by and accepts these Terms and Conditions of Auction ("Bidder(s)").
5. All Bidders must meet Auctioneer's qualifications to bid. Any Bidder who is not a client in good standing of the Auctioneer may be disqualified at Auctioneer's sole option and will not be awarded lots. Such determination may be made by Auctioneer in its sole and unlimited discretion, at any time prior to, during, or even after the close of the Auction. Auctioneer reserves the right to exclude any person from the auction.
6. If an entity places a bid, then the person executing the bid on behalf of the entity agrees to personally guarantee payment for any successful bid.

Credit:

7. In order to place bids, Bidders who have not established credit with the Auctioneer must either furnish satisfactory credit information (including two collectibles-related business references) or supply valid credit card information along with a social security number, well in advance of the Auction. Bids placed through our Interactive Internet program will only be accepted from pre-registered Bidders. Bidders who are not members of HA.com or affiliates should preregister at least 48 hours before the start of the first session (exclusive of holidays or weekends) to allow adequate time to contact references. Credit will be granted at the discretion of Auctioneer. Additionally Bidders who have not previously established credit or who wish to bid in excess of their established credit history may be required to provide their social security number or the last four digits thereof so a credit check may be performed prior to Auctioneer's acceptance of a bid. Check writing privileges and immediate delivery of merchandise may also be determined by pre-approval of credit based on a combination of criteria: HA.com history, related industry references, bank verification, a credit bureau report and/or a personal guarantee for a corporate or partnership entity in advance of the auction venue.

Bidding Options:

8. Bids in Signature® Auctions or Grand Format Auctions may be placed as set forth in the printed catalog section entitled "Choose your bidding method." For auctions held solely on the Internet, see the alternatives on HA.com. Review at HA.com/common/howtobid.php.
9. Presentment of Bids: Non-Internet bids (including but not limited to podium, fax, phone and mail bids) are treated similar to floor bids in that they must be on-increment or at a half increment (called a cut bid). Any podium, fax, phone, or mail bids that do not conform to a full or half increment will be rounded up or down to the nearest full or half increment and this revised amount will be considered your high bid.
10. Auctioneer's Execution of Certain Bids. Auctioneer cannot be responsible for your errors in bidding, so carefully check that every bid is entered correctly. When identical mail or FAX bids are submitted, preference is given to the first received. To ensure the greatest accuracy, your written bids should be entered on the standard printed bid sheet and be received at Auctioneer's place of business at least two business days before the Auction start. Auctioneer is not responsible for executing mail bids or FAX bids received on or after the day the first lot is sold, nor Internet bids submitted after the published closing time; nor is Auctioneer responsible for proper execution of bids submitted by telephone, mail, FAX, e-mail, Internet, or in person once the Auction begins. Bids placed electronically via the internet may not be withdrawn until your written request is received and acknowledged by Auctioneer (FAX: 214-443-8425); such requests must state the reason, and may constitute grounds for withdrawal of bidding privileges. Lots won by mail Bidders will not be delivered at the Auction unless prearranged.
11. Caveat as to Bid Increments. Bid increments (over the current bid level) determine the lowest amount you may bid on a particular lot. Bids greater than one increment over the current bid can be any whole dollar amount. It is possible under several circumstances for winning bids to be between increments, sometimes only $1 above the previous increment. Please see: "How can I lose by less than an increment?" on our website. Bids will be accepted in whole dollar amounts only. No "buy" or "unlimited" bids will be accepted.

The following chart governs current bidding increments for Signature auctions; Internet-only auction bidding increments are approximately half of these amounts (see HA.com/c/ref/web-tips.zx#guidelines-increments).

Current Bid	Bid Increment	Current Bid	Bid Increment
< - $10	$1	$10,000 - $19,999	$1,000
$10 - $29	$2	$20,000 - $29,999	$2,000
$30 - $49	$3	$30,000 - $49,999	$2,500
$50 - $99	$5	$50,000 - $99,999	$5,000
$100 - $199	$10	$100,000 - $199,999	$10,000
$200 - $299	$20	$200,000 - $299,999	$20,000
$300 - $499	$25	$300,000 - $499,999	$25,000
$500 - $999	$50	$500,000 - $999,999	$50,000
$1,000 - $1,999	$100	$1,000,000 - $4,999,999	$100,000
$2,000 - $2,999	$200	$5,000,000- $9,999,999	$250,000
$3,000 - $4,999	$250	>$10,000,000	$500,000
$5,000 - $9,999	$500		

12. If Auctioneer calls for a full increment, a bidder may request Auctioneer to accept a bid at half of the increment ("Cut Bid") only once per lot. After offering a Cut Bid, bidders may continue to participate only at full increments. Off-increment bids may be accepted by the Auctioneer at Signature® Auctions and Grand Format Auctions. If the Auctioneer solicits bids other than the expected increment, these bids will not be considered Cut Bids.

Conducting the Auction:

13. Notice of the consignor's liberty to place bids on his lots in the Auction is hereby made in accordance with Article 2 of the Texas Business and Commercial Code. A "Minimum Bid" is an amount below which the lot will not sell. THE CONSIGNOR OF PROPERTY MAY PLACE WRITTEN "Minimum Bids" ON HIS LOTS IN ADVANCE OF THE AUCTION; ON SUCH LOTS, IF THE HAMMER PRICE DOES NOT MEET THE "Minimum Bid", THE CONSIGNOR MAY PAY A REDUCED COMMISSION ON THOSE LOTS. "Minimum Bids" are generally posted online several days prior to the Auction closing. For any successful bid placed by a consignor on his Property on the Auction floor, or by any means during the live session, or after the "Minimum Bid" for an Auction have been posted, we will require the consignor to pay full Buyer's Premium and Seller's Commissions on such lot.
14. The highest qualified Bidder recognized by the Auctioneer shall be the Buyer. In the event of a tie bid, the earliest bid received or recognized wins. In the event of any dispute between any Bidders at an Auction, Auctioneer may at his sole discretion reoffer the lot. Auctioneer's decision and declaration of the winning Bidder shall be final and binding upon all Bidders. Bids properly offered, whether by floor Bidder or other means of bidding, may on occasion be missed or go unrecognized; in such cases, the Auctioneer may declare the recognized bid accepted as the winning bid, regardless of whether a competing bid may have been higher. Auctioneer reserves the right after the hammer fall to accept bids and reopen bidding for bids placed through the Internet or otherwise.
15. Auctioneer reserves the right to refuse to honor any bid or to limit the amount of any bid, in its sole discretion. A bid is considered not made in "Good Faith" when made by an insolvent or irresponsible person, a person under the age of eighteen, or is not supported by satisfactory credit, collectibles references, or otherwise. Regardless of the disclosure of his identity, any bid by a consignor or his agent on a lot consigned by him is deemed to be made in "Good Faith." Any person apparently appearing on the OFAC list is not eligible to bid.
16. Nominal Bids. The Auctioneer in its sole discretion may reject nominal bids, small opening bids, or very nominal advances. If a lot bearing estimates fails to open for 40–60% of the low estimate, the Auctioneer may pass the item or may place a protective bid on behalf of the consignor.
17. Lots bearing bidding estimates shall open at Auctioneer's discretion (approximately 50%-60% of the low estimate). In the event that no bid meets or exceeds that opening amount, the lot shall pass as unsold.
18. All items are to be purchased per lot as numerically indicated and no lots will be broken. Auctioneer reserves the right to withdraw, prior to the close, any lots from the Auction.
19. Auctioneer reserves the right to rescind the sale in the event of nonpayment, breach of a warranty, disputed ownership, auctioneer's clerical error or omission in exercising bids and reserves, or for any other reason and in Auctioneer's sole discretion. In cases of nonpayment, Auctioneer's election to void a sale does not relieve the Bidder from their obligation to pay Auctioneer its fees (seller's and buyer's premium) and any other damages or expenses pertaining to the lot.
20. Auctioneer occasionally experiences Internet and/or Server service outages, and Auctioneer periodically schedules system downtime for maintenance and other purposes, during which Bidders cannot participate or place bids. If such outages occur, we may at our discretion extend bidding for the Auction. Bidders unable to place their Bids through the Internet are directed to contact Client Services at 877-HERITAGE (437-4824).
21. The Auctioneer, its affiliates, or their employees consign items to be sold in the Auction, and may bid on those lots or any other lots. Auctioneer or affiliates expressly reserve the right to modify any such bids at any time prior to the hammer based upon data made known to the Auctioneer or its affiliates. The Auctioneer may extend advances, guarantees, or loans to certain consignors.
22. The Auctioneer has the right to sell certain unsold items after the close of the Auction. Such lots shall be considered sold during the Auction and all these Terms and Conditions shall apply to such sales including but not limited to the Buyer's Premium, return rights, and disclaimers.

Payment:

23. All sales are strictly for cash in United States dollars (including U.S. currency, bank wire, cashier checks, travelers checks, eChecks, and bank money orders, and are subject to all reporting requirements). All deliveries are subject to good funds; funds being received in Auctioneer's account before delivery of the Purchases; and all payments are subject to a clearing period. Auctioneer reserves the right to determine if a check constitutes "good funds": checks drawn on a U.S. bank are subject to a ten business day hold, and thirty days when drawn on an international bank. Clients with pre-arranged credit status may receive immediate credit for payments via eCheck, personal or corporate checks. All others will be subject to a hold of 5 days, or more, for the funds to clear prior to releasing merchandise. (ref. T&C item 7 Credit for additional information.) Payments can be made 24-48 hours post auction from the My Orders page of the HA.com website.
24. Payment is due upon closing of the Auction session, or upon presentment of an invoice. Auctioneer reserves the right to void an invoice if payment in full is not received within 7 days after the close of the Auction. In cases of nonpayment, Auctioneer's election to void a sale does not relieve the Bidder from their obligation to pay Auctioneer its fees (seller's and buyer's premium) on the lot and any other damages pertaining to the lot.
25. Lots delivered to you, or your representative in the States of Texas, California, New York, or other states where the Auction may be held, are subject to all applicable state and local taxes, unless appropriate permits are on file with Auctioneer. (Note: Coins are only subject to sales tax in California on invoices under $1500 and there is no sales tax on coins in Texas) Bidder agrees to pay Auctioneer the actual amount of tax due in the event that sales tax is not properly collected due to: 1) an expired, inaccurate, inappropriate tax certificate or declaration, 2) an incorrect interpretation of the applicable statute, 3) or any other reason. The appropriate form or certificate must be on file at and verified by Auctioneer five days prior to Auction or tax must be paid; only if such form or certificate is received by Auctioneer within 4 days after the Auction can a refund of tax paid be made. Lots from different Auctions may not be aggregated for sales tax purposes..
26. In the event that a Bidder's payment is dishonored upon presentment(s), Bidder shall pay the maximum statutory processing fee set by applicable state law. If you attempt to pay via eCheck and your financial institution denies this transfer from your bank account, or the payment cannot be completed using the selected funding source, you agree to complete payment using your credit card on file.
27. If any Auction invoice submitted by Auctioneer is not paid in full when due, the unpaid balance will bear interest at the highest rate permitted by law from the date of invoice until paid. Any invoice not paid when due will bear a three percent (3%) late fee on the invoice amount or three percent (3%) of any installment that is past due. If the Auctioneer refers any invoice to an attorney for collection, the buyer agrees to pay attorney's fees, court costs, and other collection costs incurred by Auctioneer. If Auctioneer assigns collection to its in-house legal staff, such attorney's time expended on the matter shall be compensated at a rate comparable to the hourly rate of independent attorneys.
28. In the event a successful Bidder fails to pay any amounts due, Auctioneer reserves the right to sell the lot(s) securing the invoice to any underbidders in the Auction that the lot(s) appeared, or at subsequent private or public sale, or relist the lot(s) in a future auction conducted by Auctioneer. A defaulting Bidder agrees to pay for the reasonable costs of resale (including a 10% seller's commission, if consigned to an auction conducted by Auctioneer). The defaulting Bidder is liable to pay any difference between his total original invoice for the lot(s), plus any applicable interest, and the net proceeds for the lot(s) if sold at private sale or the subsequent hammer price of the lot(s) less the 10% seller's commissions, if sold at an Auctioneer's auction.
29. Auctioneer reserves the right to require payment in full in good funds before delivery of the merchandise.
30. Auctioneer shall have a lien against the merchandise purchased by the buyer to secure payment of the Auction invoice. Auctioneer is further granted a lien and the right to retain possession of any other property of the buyer then held by the Auctioneer or its affiliates to secure payment of any Auction invoice or any other amounts due the Auctioneer or affiliates from the buyer. With respect to these lien rights, Auctioneer shall have all the rights of a secured creditor

under Article 9 of the Texas Uniform Commercial Code, including but not limited to the right of sale. In addition, with respect to payment of the Auction invoice(s), the buyer waives any and all rights of offset he might otherwise have against the Auctioneer and the consignor of the merchandise included on the invoice. If a Bidder owes Auctioneer or its affiliates on any account, Auctioneer and its affiliates shall have the right to offset such unpaid account by any credit balance due Bidder, and it may secure by possessory lien any unpaid amount by any of the Bidder's property in their possession.

31. Title shall not pass to the successful Bidder until all invoices are paid in full. It is the responsibility of the buyer to provide adequate insurance coverage for the items once they have been delivered to a common carrier or third-party shipper.

Delivery; Shipping; and Handling Charges:

32. Buyer is liable for shipping and handling. Please refer to Auctioneer's website www.HA.com/common/shipping.php for the latest charges or call Auctioneer. Auctioneer is unable to combine purchases from other auctions or affiliates into one package for shipping purposes. Lots won will be shipped in a commercially reasonable time after payment in good funds for the merchandise and the shipping fees is received or credit extended, except when third-party shipment occurs. Buyer agrees that Service and Handling charges related to shipping items which are not pre-paid may be charged to the credit card on file with Auctioneer.
33. Successful international Bidders shall provide written shipping instructions, including specified customs declarations, to the Auctioneer for any lots to be delivered outside of the United States. NOTE: Declaration value shall be the item'(s) hammer price together with its buyer's premium and Auctioneer shall use the correct harmonized code for the lot. Domestic Buyers on lots designated for third-party shipment must designate the common carrier, accept risk of loss, and prepay shipping costs.
34. All shipping charges will be borne by the successful Bidder. On all domestic shipments, any risk of loss during shipment will be borne by Heritage until the shipping carrier's confirmation of delivery to the address of record in Auctioneer's file (carrier's confirmation is conclusive to prove delivery to Bidder; if the client has a Signature release on file with the carrier, the package is considered delivered without Signature) or delivery by Heritage to Bidder's selected third-party shipper. On all foreign shipments, any risk of loss during shipment will be borne by the Bidder following Auctioneer's delivery to the Bidder's designated common carrier or third-party shipper.
35. Due to the nature of some items sold, it shall be the responsibility for the successful Bidder to arrange pick-up and shipping through third-parties; as to such items Auctioneer shall have no liability. Failure to pick-up or arrange shipping in a timely fashion (within ten days) shall subject Lots to storage and moving charges, including a $100 administration fee plus $10 daily storage for larger items and $5.00 daily for smaller items (storage fee per item) after 35 days. In the event the Lot is not removed within ninety days, the Lot may be offered for sale to recover any past due storage or moving fees, including a 10% Seller's Commission.

36A. The laws of various countries regulate the import or export of certain plant and animal properties, including (but not limited to) items made of (or including) ivory, whalebone, turtle shell, coral, crocodile, or other wildlife. Transport of such lots may require special licenses for export, import, or both. Bidder is responsible for: 1) obtaining all information on such restricted items for both export and import; 2) obtaining all such licenses and/or permits. Delay or failure to obtain any such license or permit does not relieve the buyer of timely compliance with standard payment terms. For further information, please contact Ron Brackemyre at 800- 872-6467 ext. 1312.

36B. Auctioneer shall not be liable for any loss caused by or resulting from:
   a. Seizure or destruction under quarantine or Customs regulation, or confiscation by order of any Government or public authority, or risks of contraband or illegal transportation of trade, or
   b. Breakage of statuary, marble, glassware, bric-a-brac, porcelains, jewelry, and similar fragile articles

37. Any request for shipping verification for undelivered packages must be made within 30 days of shipment by Auctioneer.

Cataloging, Warranties and Disclaimers:

38. NO WARRANTY, WHETHER EXPRESSED OR IMPLIED, IS MADE WITH RESPECT TO ANY DESCRIPTION CONTAINED IN THIS AUCTION OR ANY SECOND OPINE. Any description of the items or second opine contained in this Auction is for the sole purpose of identifying the items for those Bidders who do not have the opportunity to view the lots prior to bidding, and no description of items has been made part of the basis of the bargain or has created any express warranty that the goods would conform to any description made by Auctioneer. Color variations can be expected in any electronic or printed imaging, and are not grounds for the return of any lot. NOTE: Auctioneer, in specified auction venues, for example, Fine Art, may have express written warranties and you are referred to those specific terms and conditions. .
39. Auctioneer is selling only such right or title to the items being sold as Auctioneer may have by virtue of consignment agreements on the date of auction and disclaims any warranty of title to the Property. Auctioneer disclaims any warranty of merchantability or fitness for any particular purposes. All images, descriptions, sales data, and archival records are the exclusive property of Auctioneer, and may be used by Auctioneer for advertising, promotion, archival records, and any other uses deemed appropriate.
40. Translations of foreign language documents may be provided as a convenience to interested parties. Auctioneer makes no representation as to the accuracy of those translations and will not be held responsible for errors in bidding arising from inaccuracies in translation.
41. Auctioneer disclaims all liability for damages, consequential or otherwise, arising out of or in connection with the sale of any Property by Auctioneer to Bidder. No third party may rely on any benefit of these Terms and Conditions and any rights, if any, established hereunder are personal to the Bidder and may not be assigned. Any statement made by the Auctioneer is an opinion and does not constitute a warranty or representation. No employee of Auctioneer may alter these Terms and Conditions, and, unless signed by a principal of Auctioneer, any such alteration is null and void.
42. Auctioneer shall not be liable for breakage of glass or damage to frames (patent or latent); such defects, in any event, shall not be a basis for any claim for return or reduction in purchase price.

Release:

43. In consideration of participation in the Auction and the placing of a bid, Bidder expressly releases Auctioneer, its officers, directors and employees, its affiliates, and its outside experts that provide second opines, from any and all claims, cause of action, chose of action, whether at law or equity or any arbitration or mediation rights existing under the rules of any professional society or affiliation based upon the assigned description, or a derivative theory, breach of warranty express or implied, representation or other matter set forth within these Terms and Conditions of Auction or otherwise. In the event of a claim, Bidder agrees that such rights and privileges conferred therein are strictly construed as specifically declared herein; e.g., authenticity, typographical error, etc. and are the exclusive remedy. Bidder, by non-compliance to these express terms of a granted remedy, shall waive any claim against Auctioneer.
44. Notice: Some Property sold by Auctioneer are inherently dangerous e.g. firearms, cannons, and small items that may be swallowed or ingested or may have latent defects all of which may cause harm to a person. Purchaser accepts all risk of loss or damage from its purchase of these items and Auctioneer disclaims any liability whether under contract or tort for damages and losses, direct or inconsequential, and expressly disclaims any warranty as to safety or usage of any lot sold.

Dispute Resolution and Arbitration Provision:

45. By placing a bid or otherwise participating in the auction, Bidder accepts these Terms and Conditions of Auction, and specifically agrees to the dispute resolution provided herein. Consumer disputes shall be resolved through court litigation which has an exclusive Dallas, Texas venue clause and jury waiver. Non-consumer dispute shall be determined in binding arbitration which arbitration replaces the right to go to court, including the right to a jury trial.
46. Auctioneer in no event shall be responsible for consequential damages, incidental damages, compensatory damages, or any other damages arising or claimed to be arising from the auction of any lot. In the event that Auctioneer cannot deliver the lot or subsequently it is established that the lot lacks title, or other transfer or condition issue is claimed, in such cases the sole remedy shall be limited to rescission of sale and refund of the amount paid by Bidder; in no case shall Auctioneer's maximum liability exceed the high bid on that lot, which bid shall be deemed for all purposes the value of the lot. After one year has elapsed, Auctioneer's maximum liability shall be limited to any commissions and fees Auctioneer earned on that lot.
47. In the event of an attribution error, Auctioneer may at its sole discretion, correct the error on the Internet, or, if discovered at a later date, to refund the buyer's purchase price without further obligation.
48. Exclusive Dispute Resolution Process: All claims, disputes, or controversies in connection with, relating to and /or arising out of your Participation in the Auction or purchase of any lot, any interpretation of the Terms and Conditions of Sale or any amendments thereto, any description of any lot or condition report, any damage to any lot, any alleged verbal modification of any term of sale or condition report or description and/or any purported settlement whether asserted in contract, tort, under Federal or State statute or regulation or any claim made by you of a lot or your Participation in the auction involving the auction or a specific lot involving a warranty or representation of a consignor or other person or entity including Auctioneer { which claim you consent to be made a party} (collectively, "Claim") shall be exclusively heard by, and the claimant (or respondent as the case may be) and Heritage each consent to the Claim being presented in a confidential binding arbitration before a single arbitrator administrated by and conducted under the rules of, the American Arbitration Association. The locale for all such arbitrations shall be Dallas, Texas. The arbitrator's award may be enforced in any court of competent jurisdiction. If a Claim involves a consumer, exclusive subject matter jurisdiction for the Claim is in the State District Courts of Dallas County, Texas and the consumer consents to subject matter and in personam jurisdiction; further CONSUMER EXPRESSLY WAIVES ANY RIGHT TO TRIAL BY JURY. A consumer may elect arbitration as specified above. Any claim involving the purchase or sale of numismatic or related items may be submitted through binding PNG arbitration. Any Claim must be brought within two (2) years of the alleged breach, default or misrepresentation or the Claim is waived. Exemplary or punitive damages are not permitted and are waived. A Claim is not subject to class certification. Nothing herein shall be construed to extend the time of return or conditions and restrictions for return. This Agreement and any Claim shall be determined and construed under Texas law. The prevailing party (a party that is awarded substantial and material relief on its damage claim based on damages sought vs. awarded or the successful defense of a Claim based on damages sought vs. awarded) may be awarded its reasonable attorneys' fees and costs.
49. No claims of any kind can be considered after the settlements have been made with the consignors. Any dispute after the settlement date is strictly between the Bidder and consignor without involvement or responsibility of the Auctioneer.
50. In consideration of their participation in or application for the Auction, a person or entity (whether the successful Bidder, a Bidder, a purchaser and/or other Auction participant or registrant) agrees that all disputes in any way relating to, arising under, connected with, or incidental to these Terms and Conditions and purchases, or default in payment thereof, shall be arbitrated pursuant to the arbitration provision. In the event that any matter including actions to compel arbitration, construe the agreement, actions in aid or arbitration or otherwise needs to be litigated, such litigation shall be exclusively in the Courts of the State of Texas, in Dallas County, Texas, and if necessary the corresponding appellate courts. For such actions, the successful Bidder, purchaser, or Auction participant also expressly submits himself to the personal jurisdiction of the State of Texas.
51. These Terms & Conditions provide specific remedies for occurrences in the auction and delivery process. Where such remedies are afforded, they shall be interpreted strictly. Bidder agrees that any claim shall utilize such remedies; Bidder making a claim in excess of those remedies provided in these Terms and Conditions agrees that in no case whatsoever shall Auctioneer's maximum liability exceed the high bid on that lot, which bid shall be deemed for all purposes the value of the lot.

Miscellaneous:

52. Agreements between Bidders and consignors to effectuate a non-sale of an item at Auction, inhibit bidding on a consigned item to enter into a private sale agreement for said item, or to utilize the Auctioneer's Auction to obtain sales for non-selling consigned items subsequent to the Auction, are strictly prohibited. If a subsequent sale of a previously consigned item occurs in violation of this provision, Auctioneer reserves the right to charge Bidder the applicable Buyer's Premium and consignor a Seller's Commission as determined for each auction venue and by the terms of the seller's agreement.
53. Acceptance of these Terms and Conditions qualifies Bidder as a client who has consented to be contacted by Heritage in the future. In conformity with "do-not-call" regulations promulgated by the Federal or State regulatory agencies, participation by the Bidder is affirmative consent to being contacted at the phone number shown in his application and this consent shall remain in effect until it is revoked in writing. Heritage may from time to time contact Bidder concerning sale, purchase, and auction opportunities available through Heritage and its affiliates and subsidiaries.
54. Rules of Construction: Auctioneer presents properties in a number of collectible fields, and as such, specific venues have promulgated supplemental Terms and Conditions. Nothing herein shall be construed to waive the general Terms and Conditions of Auction by these additional rules and shall be construed to give force and effect to the rules in their entirety.

State Notices:

Notice as to an Auction in California. Auctioneer has in compliance with Title 2.95 of the California Civil Code as amended October 11, 1993 Sec. 1812.600, posted with the California Secretary of State its bonds for it and its employees, and the auction is being conducted in compliance with Sec. 2338 of the Commercial Code and Sec. 535 of the Penal Code.

Notice as to an Auction in New York City. These Terms and Conditions of Sale are designed to conform to the applicable sections of the New York City Department of Consumer Affairs Rules and Regulations as Amended. This sale is a Public Auction Sale conducted by Heritage Auctioneers & Galleries, Inc. # 41513036. The New York City licensed auctioneers are: Sam Foose, #095260; Kathleen Guzman, #0762165; Nicholas Dawes, #1304724; Ed Beardsley, #1183220; Scott Peterson, #1306933; Andrea Voss, #1320558, who will conduct the Sale on behalf of itself and Heritage Numismatic Auctions, Inc. (for Coins) and Currency Auctions of America, Inc. (for currency). All lots are subject to: the consignor's rights to bid thereon in accord with these Terms and Conditions of Sale, consignor's option to receive advances on their consignments, and Auctioneer, in its sole discretion, may offer limited extended financing to registered bidders, in accord with Auctioneer's internal credit standards. A registered bidder may inquire whether a lot is subject to an advance or a reserve. Auctioneer has made advances to various consignors in this sale. On lots bearing an estimate, the term refers to a value range placed on an item by the Auctioneer in its sole opinion but the final price is determined by the bidders.

Notice as to an Auction in Texas. In compliance with TDLR rule 67.100(c)(1), notice is hereby provided that this auction is covered by a Recovery Fund administered by the Texas Department of Licensing and Regulation, P.O. Box 12157, Austin, Texas 78711 (512) 463-6599. Any complaints may be directed to the same address.

Notice as to an Auction in Ohio: Auction firm and Auctioneer are licensed by the Dept. of Agriculture, and either the licensee is bonded in favor of the state or an aggrieved person may initiate a claim against the auction recovery fund created in Section 4707.25 of the Revised Code as a result of the licensee's actions, whichever is applicable.

Terms and Conditions of Auction

SPORTS COLLECTIBLES TERM A: Signature. Auctions are not on approval. No certified material may be returned because of possible differences of opinion with respect to the grade offered by any third-party organization, dealer, or service. No guarantee of grade is offered for uncertified Property sold and subsequently submitted to a third-party grading service. There are absolutely no exceptions to this policy. Under extremely limited circumstances, (e.g. gross cataloging error) a purchaser, who did not bid from the floor, may request Auctioneer to evaluate voiding a sale; such request must be made in writing detailing the alleged gross error, and submission of the lot to the Auctioneer must be pre-approved by the Auctioneer; A bidder must notify the appropriate department head (check the inside front cover of the catalog or our website for a listing of department heads) in writing of such request within three (3) days of the mail bidder's receipt of the lot. Any lot that is to be evaluated must be in our offices within 30 days after Auction. Grading does not qualify for this evaluation process nor do such complaints constitute a basis to challenge the authenticity of a lot. AFTER THAT 30-DAY PERIOD, NO LOTS MAY BE RETURNED FOR REASONS OTHER THAN AUTHENTICITY. Lots returned must be housed intact in the original holder. No lots purchased by floor Bidders (including those Bidders acting as agents for others) may be returned. Late remittance for purchases may be considered just cause to revoke all return privileges.

SPORTS COLLECTIBLES TERM B: Auctions conducted solely on the Internet THREE (3) DAY RETURN POLICY. All lots paid for within seven days of the Internet-only Auction closing are sold with a three (3) day return privilege. You may return lots under the following conditions: Within three days of receipt of the lot, you must first notify Auctioneer by contacting Client Service by phone (877-HERITAGE (437-4824)) or e-mail (Bid@HA.com), and immediately mail the lot(s) fully insured to the attention of Returns, Heritage, 3500 Maple Avenue, 17th Floor, Dallas TX 75219-3941. Lots must be housed intact in their original holder and condition. You are responsible for the insured, safe delivery of any lots. A non-negotiable return fee of 5% of the purchase price ($10 per lot minimum) will be deducted from the refund for each returned lot or billed directly. Postage and handling fees are not refunded. After the three-day period (from receipt), no items may be returned for any reason. Late remittance for purchases revokes all Return privileges.

SPORTS COLLECTIBLES TERM C: Bidders who have inspected the lots or had the opportunity to Inspect the lots prior to any Auction will not be granted any return privileges.

SPORTS COLLECTIBLES TERM D: Sportscards sold referencing a third-party grading service are sold "as is" without any express or implied warranty. Certain warranties may be available from the grading services and the Bidder is referred to them for further details: Professional Sports Authenticator (PSA), P.O. Box 6180 Newport Beach, CA 92658; Sportscard Guaranty LLC (SGC) P.O. Box 6919 Parsippany, NJ 07054-6919; Global Authentication (GAI), P.O. Box 57042 Irvine, Ca. 92619; Beckett Grading Service (BGS), 15850 Dallas Parkway, Dallas TX 75248.

SPORTS COLLECTIBLES TERM E: On any lot presented with a Letter of Authenticity ("LOA") issued by Auctioneer or its Heritage affiliates, that warranty inures only to the original purchaser (as shown in Auctioneer's records) "Purchaser". Purchaser may not transfer the rights afforded under the LOA and it is null and void when Purchaser transfers or attempts to transfer the lot. The LOA warranty is valid from date of the auction in which Purchaser was awarded the lot to four (4) years after its purchase. The LOA warranty is valid as to its attribution to the person or entity described or to the lot's usage, e.g. game worn. Claim procedure: Purchaser must contact the Auctioneer prior to submission of the lot as to his intent to make a claim and arrange secure shipment. If a lot's authenticity is questioned by Purchaser within the warranty period, Purchaser must present with the claim, authoritative written evidence that the lot is not authentic as determined by a known expert in the sports field. If Auctioneer concurs that the lot is not as represented, Purchaser shall be refunded their purchase price. If the Auctioneer denies the claim, the Purchaser may file the dispute with the American Arbitration Association with locale in Dallas, Texas, before a single arbitration under expedited rules. The LOA does not provide for incidental or consequential damages or other indirect damages. Any lot sold with a certificate of authenticity or other warranty from an entity other than Auctioneer or Heritage's affiliates is subject to such issuing entity's rules and such conditions are the sole remedy afforded to purchaser. For information as to third party authentication warranties the bidder is directed to: PSA/DNA, P.O. Box 6180 Newport Beach, CA 92658 (800) 325-1121. James Spence Authentication (JSA), 2 Sylvan Way, Suite 102 Parsippany, NJ 07054 (888) 457-7362; or as otherwise noted on the Certificate.

SPORTS COLLECTIBLES TERM F: Bidders who intend to challenge authenticity or provenance of a lot must notify Auctioneer in writing within thirty (30) days of the Auction's conclusion. In the event Auctioneer cannot deliver the lot or subsequently it is established that the lot lacks title, provenance, authenticity, or other transfer or condition issue is claimed, Auctioneer's liability shall be limited to rescission of sale and refund of purchase price; in no case shall Auctioneer's maximum liability exceed the high bid on that lot, which bid shall be deemed for all purposes the value of the lot. After one year has elapsed, Auctioneer's maximum liability shall be limited to any commissions and fees Auctioneer earned on that lot.

SPORTS COLLECTIBLES TERM G: Auctioneer shall not be liable for any patent or latent defect or controversy pertaining to or arising from any encapsulated collectible. In any such instance, purchaser's remedy, if any, shall be solely against the service certifying the collectible.

SPORTS COLLECTIBLES TERM H: Due to changing grading standards over time, differing interpretations, and to possible mishandling of items by subsequent owners, Auctioneer reserves the right to grade items differently than shown on certificates from any grading service that accompany the items. Auctioneer also reserves the right to grade items differently than the grades shown in the prior catalog should such items be reconsigned to any future auction.

SPORTS COLLECTIBLES TERM I: Although consensus grading is employed by most third-party services, it should be noted as aforesaid that grading is not an exact science. In fact, it is entirely possible that if a lot is broken out of a plastic holder and resubmitted to another grading service or even to the same service, the lot could come back with a different grade assigned.

SPORTS COLLECTIBLES TERM J: Certification does not guarantee protection against the normal risks associated with potentially volatile markets. The degree of liquidity for certified collectibles will vary according to general market conditions and the particular lot involved. For some lots there may be no active market at all at certain points in time.

For wiring instructions call the Credit department at 877-HERITAGE (437-4824) or e-mail: CreditDept@HA.com

---

New York State Auctions Only

Notice as to an Auction in New York City. These Terms and Conditions of Sale are designed to conform to the applicable sections of the New York City Department of Consumer Affairs Rules and Regulations as Amended. This sale is a Public Auction Sale conducted by Heritage Auctioneers & Galleries, Inc. # 41513036. The New York City licensed auctioneers are: Sam Foose, #095260; Kathleen Guzman, #0762165; Nicholas Dawes, #1304724; Ed Beardsley, #1183220; Scott Peterson, #1306933; Andrea Voss, #1320558, Michael J. Sadler, # 1304630, who will conduct the Sale on behalf of itself and Heritage Numismatic Auctions, Inc. (for Coins) and Currency Auctions of America, Inc. (for currency). All lots are subject to: the consignor's rights to bid thereon in accord with these Terms and Conditions of Sale, consignor's option to receive advances on their consignments, and Auctioneer, in its sole discretion, may offer limited extended financing to registered bidders, in accord with Auctioneer's internal credit standards. A registered bidder may inquire whether a lot is subject to an advance or a reserve. Auctioneer has made advances to various consignors in this sale. On lots bearing an estimate, the term refers to a value range placed on an item by the Auctioneer in its sole opinion but the final price is determined by the bidders. Rev 11-19-12

Rev.7-10-2013

How to Ship Your Purchases

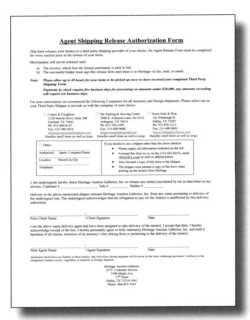

Agent Shipping Release
Authorization form

Heritage Auction Galleries requires "Third Party Shipping" for certain items in this auction not picked up in person by the buyer. It shall be the responsibility of the successful bidder to arrange pick up and shipping through a third party; as to such items auctioneer shall have no liability.

Steps to follow:

1. Select a shipping company from the list below or a company of your choosing which will remain on file and in effect until you advise otherwise in writing.

2. Complete, sign, and return an Agent Shipping Release Authorization form to Heritage (this form will automatically be emailed to you along with your winning bid(s) notice or may be obtained by calling Client Services at 866-835-3243). The completed form may be faxed to 214-409-1425.

3. Heritage Auctions' shipping department will coordinate with the shipping company you have selected to pick up your purchases.

Shippers that Heritage has used are listed below. However, you are not obligated to choose from the following and may provide Heritage with information of your preferred shipper.

Navis Pack & Ship
11009 Shady Trail
Dallas, TX 75229
Ph: 972-870-1212
Fax: 214-409-9001
Navis.Dallas@GoNavis.com

The Packing & Moving Center
2040 E. Arkansas Lane, Ste #222
Arlington, TX 76011
Ph: 817-795-1999
Fax: 214-409-9000
thepackman@sbcglobal.net

Craters & Freighters
2220 Merritt Drive, Suite 200
Garland, TX 75041
Ph: 972-840-8147
Fax: 214-780-5674
dallas@cratersandfreighters.com

- It is the Third Party Shipper's responsibility to pack (or crate) and ship (or freight) your purchase to you. Please make all payment arrangements for shipping with your Shipper of choice.

- Any questions concerning Third Party Shipping can be addressed through our Client Services Department at 1-866-835-3243.

- Successful bidders are advised that pick-up or shipping arrangements should be made within ten (10) days of the auction or they may be subject to storage fees as stated in Heritage's Terms & Conditions of Auction, item 35.

NOTICE of CITES COMPLIANCE; When purchasing items made from protected species.
Any property made of or incorporating endangered or protected species or wildlife may have import and export restrictions established by the Convention on International Trade in Endangered Species of Wild Fauna and Flora (CITES). These items are not available to ship Internationally or in some cases, domestically. By placing a bid the bidder acknowledges that he is aware of the restriction and takes responsibility in obtaining and paying for any license or permits relevant to delivery of the product. Lots containing potentially regulated wildlife material are noted in the description as a convenience to our clients. Heritage Auctions does not accept liability for errors or for failure to mark lots containing protected or regulated species.

EVERY YEAR HERITAGE ALSO
HOLDS THREE SIGNATURE® VINTAGE
MOVIE POSTER AUCTIONS

Consign your valuable poster collection now.

Additionally, be sure to check out our weekly Sunday Internet Movie Poster Auctions all year long. To view lots and bid online visit HA.com/MoviePosters.

Bidding is easy, by postal mail, fax, email, phone, through our website at HA.com, or via our interactive live bidding platform, HERITAGE Live!® Check out the auctions online, where you'll find full-color, enlargeable images of each and every lot, as well as our complete and informative catalog descriptions.

Dracula (Universal, 1931).
One Sheet (27" X 41") Style F.
Realized: $310,700
March 2009

To consign to
an upcoming
auction, contact:
GREY SMITH
Director, Movie
Poster Auctions
214-409-1367
GreySm@HA.com

King Kong (RKO, 1933).
Three Sheet (40.25" X 79") St
Realized: $388,375
November 2012

Free catalog and *The Collector's Handbook* ($65 value) for new clients. Please submit auction invoices of $1000+ in this category, from any source. Include your contact information and mail to Her fax 214-409-1425, email catalogorders@HA.com, or call 866-835-3243. For more details, go to HA.com/FCO.

Annual Sales Exceed $800 Million I 800,000+ Online Bidder-Members

500 Maple Ave. I Dallas, TX 75219 I 877-HERITAGE (437-4824) I HA.com

DALLAS I NEW YORK I BEVERLY HILLS I SAN FRANCISCO I HOUSTON I PARIS I GENEVA

THE WORLD'S LARGEST COLLECTIBLES AUC

HERITAGE
AUCTIONS

HA.com/FBMoviePosters HA.com

& NY Auctioneer license: Samuel Foose 11727 & 0952360. Heritage Auction Galleries CA Bond #RSB2004175;

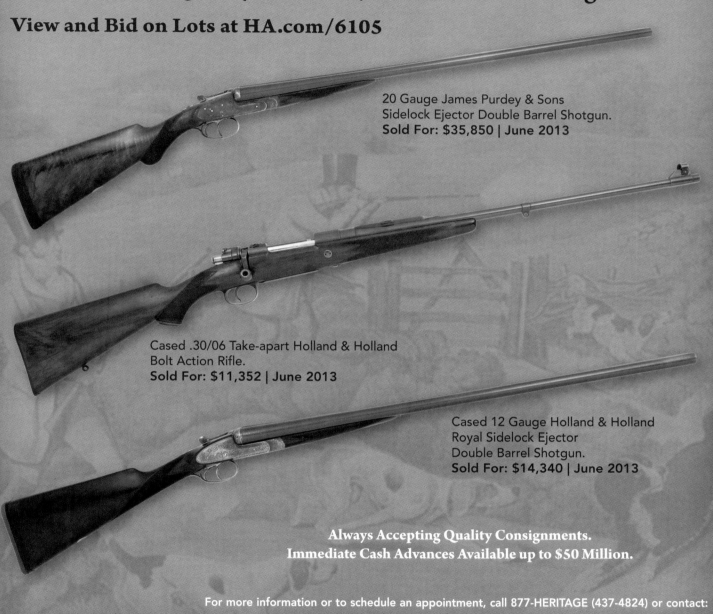

Department Specialists

For the extensions below, please dial 877-HERITAGE (437-4824)

Comics & Comic Art
HA.com/Comics

Ed Jaster, Ext. 1288 • EdJ@HA.com
Lon Allen, Ext. 1261 • LonA@HA.com
Steve Borock, Ext. 1337 • SteveB@HA.com
Barry Sandoval, Ext. 1377 • BarryS@HA.com
Todd Hignite, Ext. 1790 • ToddH@HA.com

Animation Art
Jim Lentz, Ext. 1991 • JimL@HA.com

Entertainment & Music Memorabilia
HA.com/Entertainment

Margaret Barrett, Ext. 1912 • MargaretB@HA.com **
John Hickey, Ext. 1264 • JohnH@HA.com
Garry Shrum, Ext. 1585 • GarryS@HA.com

Vintage Guitars & Musical Instruments
HA.com/Guitar

Mike Gutierrez, Ext. 1183 • MikeG@HA.com
Isaiah Evans, Ext. 1201 • IsaiahE@HA.com

Fine Art

American Indian Art
HA.com/AmericanIndian
Delia Sullivan, Ext. 1343 • DeliaS@HA.com

American, Western & European Art
HA.com/FineArt

Ed Jaster, Ext. 1288 • EdJ@HA.com *
Brian Roughton, Ext. 1210 • BrianR@HA.com
Marianne Berardi, Ph.D., Ext. 1506 • MarianneB@HA.com
Ariana Hartsock, Ext. 1283 • ArianaH@HA.com
Kirsty Buchanan, Ext. 1741 • KirstyB@HA.com
Aviva Lehmann, Ext. 1519 • AvivaL@HA.com *

California Art
HA.com/FineArt
Alissa Ford, Ext. 1926 • AlissaF@HA.com ***

Decorative Arts & Design
HA.com/Decorative
Karen Rigdon, Ext. 1723 • KarenR@HA.com
Carolyn Mani, Ext. 1677 • CarolynM@HA.com **

Illustration Art
HA.com/Illustration
Ed Jaster, Ext. 1288 • EdJ@HA.com *
Todd Hignite, Ext. 1790 • ToddH@HA.com

Lalique & Art Glass
HA.com/Design
Nicholas Dawes, Ext. 1605 • NickD@HA.com *

Modern & Contemporary Art
HA.com/Modern
Frank Hettig, Ext. 1157 • FrankH@HA.com
Brandon Kennedy, Ext. 1965 • BrandonK@HA.com

Photographs
HA.com/Photographs
Ed Jaster, Ext. 1288 • EdJ@HA.com
Rachel Peart, Ext. 1625 • RPeart@HA.com

Silver & Vertu
HA.com/Silver
Karen Rigdon, Ext. 1723 • KarenR@HA.com

Texas Art
HA.com/TexasArt
Atlee Phillips, Ext. 1786 • AtleeP@HA.com

Handbags & Luxury Accessories
HA.com/Luxury
Matt Rubinger, Ext. 1419 • Matt@HA.com
Caitlin Donovan, Ext. 1478 • CaitlinD@HA.com

Historical

Americana & Political
HA.com/Historical
Tom Slater, Ext. 1441 • TomS@HA.com
John Hickey, Ext. 1264 • JohnH@HA.com
Michael Riley, Ext. 1467 • MichaelR@HA.com
Don Ackerman, Ext. 1736 • DonA@HA.com

Arms & Armor
HA.com/Arms
Cliff Chappell, Ext. 1887 • CliffordC@HA.com ***
David Carde, Ext. 1881 • DavidC@HA.com ***

Civil War & Militaria
HA.com/CivilWar
David Carde, Ext. 1881 • DavidC@HA.com

Historical Manuscripts
HA.com/Manuscripts
Sandra Palomino, Ext. 1107 • SandraP@HA.com

Rare Books
HA.com/Books
James Gannon, Ext. 1609 • JamesG@HA.com
Joe Fay, Ext. 1544 • JoeF@HA.com

Space Exploration
HA.com/Space
John Hickey, Ext. 1264 • JohnH@HA.com
Michael Riley, Ext. 1467 • MichaelR@HA.com

Texana
HA.com/Historical
Sandra Palomino, Ext. 1107 • SandraP@HA.com

Domain Names & Intellectual Property
HA.com/IP
Aron Meystedt, Ext. 1362 • AronM@HA.com

Jewelry
HA.com/Jewelry
Jill Burgum, Ext. 1697 • JillB@HA.com
Peggy Gottlieb, Ext. 1847 • PGottlieb@HA.com **
Karen Sampieri, Ext. 1542 • KarenS@HA.com *

Luxury Real Estate
HA.com/LuxuryRealEstate
Nate Schar, Ext. 1457 • NateS@HA.com
Scott Foerst, Ext. 1521 • ScottF@HA.com

Movie Posters

HA.com/MoviePosters

Grey Smith, Ext. 1367 • GreySm@HA.com

Bruce Carteron, Ext. 1551 • BruceC@HA.com

Nature & Science

HA.com/NatureAndScience

Jim Walker, Ext. 1869 • JimW@HA.com

Mary Fong/Walker, Ext. 1870 • MaryW@HA.com

Craig Kissick, Ext. 1995 • CraigK@HA.com

Numismatics

Coins – United States

HA.com/Coins

David Mayfield, Ext. 1277 • David@HA.com

Win Callender, Ext. 1415 • WinC@HA.com

Chris Dykstra, Ext. 1380 • ChrisD@HA.com

Mark Feld, Ext. 1321 • MFeld@HA.com

Sam Foose, Ext. 1227 • Sam@HA.com

Joel Gabrelow, Ext. 1623 • JoelG@HA.com

Jason Henrichsen, Ext. 1714 • JasonH@HA.com ***

Jim Jelinski, Ext. 1257 • JimJ@HA.com

Jacob Leudecke, Ext. 1888 • JacobL@HA.com

Bob Marino, Ext. 1374 • BobMarino@HA.com

Brian Mayfield, Ext. 1668 • BMayfield@HA.com

James Mayer, Ext. 1818 • JamesM@HA.com **

Al Pinkall, Ext. 1835 • AlP@HA.com *

Robert Powell, Ext. 1837 • RobertP@HA.com

Beau Streicher, Ext. 1645 • BeauS@HA.com

Rare Currency

HA.com/Currency

Len Glazer, Ext. 1390 • Len@HA.com

Allen Mincho, Ext. 1327 • Allen@HA.com

Dustin Johnston, Ext. 1302 • Dustin@HA.com

David Liu, Ext. 1584 • DavidL@HA.com

Michael Moczalla, Ext. 1481 • MichaelM@HA.com

Jason Friedman, Ext. 1582 • JasonF@HA.com

World & Ancient Coins

HA.com/WorldCoins

Cristiano Bierrenbach, Ext. 1661 • CrisB@HA.com

Warren Tucker, Ext. 1287 • WTucker@HA.com

David Michaels, Ext. 1606 • DMichaels@HA.com **

Scott Cordry, Ext. 1369 • ScottC@HA.com

Matt Orsini, Ext. 1523 • MattO@HA.com

Sam Spiegel, Ext. 1524 • SamS@HA.com

Sports Collectibles

HA.com/Sports

Chris Ivy, Ext. 1319 • CIvy@HA.com

Peter Calderon, Ext. 1789 • PeterC@HA.com

Tony Giese, Ext. 1997 • TonyG@HA.com

Derek Grady, Ext. 1975 • DerekG@HA.com

Mike Gutierrez, Ext. 1183 • MikeG@HA.com

Lee Iskowitz, Ext. 1601 • LeeI@HA.com *

Mark Jordan, Ext. 1187 • MarkJ@HA.com

Chris Nerat, Ext. 1615 • ChrisN@HA.com

Rob Rosen, Ext. 1767 • RRosen@HA.com

Jonathan Scheier, Ext. 1314 • JonathanS@HA.com

Timepieces

HA.com/Timepieces

Jim Wolf, Ext. 1659 • JWolf@HA.com

Wine

HA.com/Wine

Frank Martell, Ext. 1753 • FrankM@HA.com

Poppy Davis, Ext. 1559 • PoppyD@HA.com

Services

Appraisal Services

HA.com/Appraisals

Meredith Meuwly, Ext. 1631• MeredithM@HA.com

Careers

HA.com/Careers

Charity Auctions

Jeri Carroll, Ext. 1873 • JeriC@HA.com

Corporate & Institutional Collections/Ventures

Erica Smith, Ext. 1828 • EricaS@HA.com

Karl Chiao, Ext. 1958 • KarlC@HA.com

Credit Department

Marti Korver, Ext. 1248 • Marti@HA.com

Media & Public Relations

Noah Fleisher, Ext. 1143 • NoahF@HA.com

Museum Services

Erica Denton, Ext. 1828 • EricaS@HA.com

Special Collections

Nicholas Dawes, Ext. 1605 • NickD@HA.com *

Trusts & Estates

HA.com/Estates

Mark Prendergast, Ext. 1632 • MPrendergast@HA.com

Karl Chiao, Ext. 1958 • KarlC@HA.com

Mimi Kapiloff, Ext. 1681 • MimiK@HA.com *

Carolyn Mani, Ext. 1677 • CarolynM@HA.com **

Locations

Dallas (World Headquarters)
214.528.3500 • 877-HERITAGE (437-4824)
3500 Maple Ave. • Dallas, TX 75219

Dallas (Fine & Decorative Arts – Design District Annex)
214.528.3500 • 877-HERITAGE (437-4824)
1518 Slocum St. • Dallas, TX 75207

New York
212.486.3500
445 Park Avenue • New York, NY 10022

Beverly Hills
310.492.8600
9478 W. Olympic Blvd.
Beverly Hills, CA 90212

San Francisco
877-HERITAGE (437-4824)
478 Jackson Street
San Francisco, CA 94111

DALLAS | NEW YORK | SAN FRANCISCO | BEVERLY HILLS | HOUSTON | PARIS | GENEVA

Corporate Officers

R. Steven Ivy, Co-Chairman

James L. Halperin, Co-Chairman

Gregory J. Rohan, President

Paul Minshull, Chief Operating Officer

Todd Imhof, Executive Vice President

Kathleen Guzman, Managing Director-New York

* Primary office location: New York
** Primary office location: Beverly Hills
*** Primary office location: San Francisco

9-23-2013

U.S. Rare Coin Auctions	Location	Auction Dates	Consignment Deadline
U.S. Rare Coins	New York	November 1-2, 2013	Closed
The Eric P. Newman Collection Part II	New York	November 15-16, 2013	Closed
U.S. Rare Coins	Houston	December 5-6, 2013	October 22, 2013

World & Ancient Coin Auctions	Location	Auction Dates	Consignment Deadline
World Coins	New York	January 5-6, 2014	November 8, 2013
The Eric P. Newman World Coin Collection	New York	January 14-15, 2014	Closed

Rare Currency Auctions	Location	Auction Dates	Consignment Deadline
Currency	Orlando	January 8-14, 2014	November 18, 2013

Fine & Decorative Arts Auctions	Location	Auction Dates	Consignment Deadline
The Estate Auction	Dallas	October 5-6, 2013	Closed
Illustration Art	New York	October 26, 2013	Closed
Photographs + Modern & Contemporary Art	Dallas	November 2, 2013	Closed
Silver & Vertu	Dallas	November 5, 2013	Closed
European Art + Western & Calif. + American Indian	Dallas	November 8-15, 2013	Closed
Texas Art	Dallas	November 16, 2013	Closed
Tiffany, Lalique & Art Glass	New York	December 4, 2013	Closed
Fine American Art	New York	December 5, 2013	Closed
The Art of New York	New York	December 5, 2013	Closed
The Estate Auction	Dallas	February 22-23, 2014	December 16, 2013
Silver & Vertu	Dallas	May 7, 2014	March 5, 2014
Illustration Art	Beverly Hills	May 8, 2014	February 28, 2014
American Indian + Western & California Art & Texas Art	Dallas	May 16-17, 2014	March 10, 2014
Modern & Contemporary Art + Photographs	Dallas	May 24, 2014	March 17, 2014
European Art	Dallas	June 6, 2014	March 31, 2014
American Art	Dallas	June 6, 2014	March 31, 2014
Decorative Art	Dallas	June 9, 2014	April 1, 2014

Jewelry, Timepieces & Luxury Accessory Auctions	Location	Auction Dates	Consignment Deadline
Timepieces	New York	November 21, 2013	Closed
Fine Jewelry + Luxury Accessories	Dallas	December 9-10, 2012	Closed
Fine Jewelry + Luxury Accessories	Dallas	Spring 2014	March 1, 2014
Timepieces	Dallas	Spring 2014	March 1, 2014

Vintage Movie Posters Auctions	Location	Auction Dates	Consignment Deadline
Vintage Movie Posters	Dallas	November 16-17, 2013	Closed
Vintage Movie Posters	Dallas	March 22-23, 2014	January 28, 2014

Comics Auctions	Location	Auction Dates	Consignment Deadline
Animation Art	Beverly Hills	November 20, 2013	October 7, 2013
Comics & Original Comic Art	Beverly Hills	November 21-22, 2013	October 8, 2013

Entertainment & Music Memorabilia Auctions	Location	Auction Dates	Consignment Deadline
Vintage Guitars & Musical Instruments	Dallas	October 25, 2013	Closed
Entertainment & Music Memorabilia	Dallas	December 6, 2013	October 15, 2013

Historical Grand Format Auctions	Location	Auction Dates	Consignment Deadline
Historical Manuscripts + Rare Books	New York	October 17-18, 2013	Closed
Space Exploration	Dallas	November 1, 2013	Closed
Americana + Legends of the Wild West	Dallas	November 23-24, 2013	October 2, 2013
Civil War & Militaria + Arms &Armor	Dallas	December 7-8, 2013	October 16, 2013
Texana	Dallas	March 8, 2014	January 15, 2014
Rare Books	Beverly Hills	February 5-6, 2014	December 15, 2013
Historical Manuscripts + Rare Books	New York	April 9-10, 2014	February 16, 2014
Space Exploration	Dallas	Spring 2014	March 1, 2014

Sports Collectibles Auctions	Location	Auction Dates	Consignment Deadline
Sports Collectibles, Golf	Dallas	December 6-7, 2013	October 15, 2013
Sports Collectibles, Platinum Night	New York	February 22-23, 2014	January 3, 2014

Nature & Science Auctions	Location	Auction Dates	Consignment Deadline
Nature & Science	Dallas	October 19-20, 2013	Closed
Nature & Science	Dallas	Spring 2014	March 1, 2014

Fine & Rare Wine	Location	Auction Dates	Consignment Deadline
Fine & Rare Wine	Beverly Hills	December 13-14, 2013	November 10, 2013

Domain Names	Location	Auction Dates	Consignment Deadline
Domain Names	New York	November 21, 2013	Closed

24329
9-30-2013

HA.com/Consign • Consignment Hotline **877-HERITAGE (437-4824)** • All dates and auctions subject to change after press time. Go to HA.com for updates.

HERITAGE INTERNET-ONLY AUCTIONS AT 10PM CT:

Comics – Sundays
Movie Posters - Sundays
Sports - Sundays
U.S. Coins - Sundays & Tuesdays
Currency – Tuesdays
Luxury Accessories - Tuesdays

Timepiece & Jewelry – Tuesdays
Modern Coins - Thursdays
Rare Books & Autographs – Thursdays
World Coins - Thursdays
Wine - 2nd Thursdays

Auctioneers: Samuel Foose: TX 11727; CA Bond #RSB2004178; FL AU1850; GA AUNR3029; IL 441001482; NC 8373; OH 2006000048; MA 03015; PA AU005443; TN 6093; WI 2230-052; NYC 0952360; Denver 1021450; Phoenix 07006332. Robert Korver: TX 13754; CA Bond #RSB2004179; FL AU2916; GA AUNR003023; IL 441001421; MA 03014; NC 8363; OH 2006000049; TN 6439; WI 2412-52; Phoenix 07102049; NYC 1096338; Denver 1021446. Teia Baber: TX 16624; CA Bond #RSB2005525. Ed Beardsley: TX Associate 16632; NYC 1183220. Nicholas Dawes: NYC 1304724. Marsha Dixey: TX 16493. Chris Dykstra: TX 16601; FL AU4069; WI 2566-052; TN 6463; IL 441001788; CA #RSB2005738. Jeff Engelken: CA Bond #RSB2004180. Alissa Ford: CA Bond #RSB2005920. NYC 1094963. Kathleen Guzman: NYC 0762165. Stewart Huckaby: TX 16590. Cindy Isennock, participating auctioneer: Baltimore Auctioneer license #AU10. Carolyn Mani: CA Bond #RSB2005661; Bob Merrill: TX 13408; MA 03022; WI 2557-052; FL AU4043; IL 441001683; CA Bond #RSB2004177. Cori Mikeals: TX 16582; CA #RSB2005645. Scott Peterson: TX 13256; NYC 1306933; IL 441001659; WI 2431-052; CA Bond #RSB2005395. Michael J. Sadler: TX 16129; FL AU3795; IL 441001478; MA 03021; TN 6487; WI 2581-052; NYC 1304630; CA Bond #RSB2005412. Andrea Voss: TX 16406; FL AU4034; MA 03019; WI 2576-052; CA Bond #RSB2004676; NYC #1320558. Jacob Walker: TX 16413; FL AU4031; WI 2567-052; IL 441001677; CA Bond #RSB2005394. (Rev.7-12)